Youth Crime and Juvenile Justice

edited by
Paul C. Friday
V. Lorne Stewart

Published in cooperation with
the American Society of Criminology

Youth Crime and Juvenile Justice

International Perspectives

PRAEGER SPECIAL STUDIES IN U.S. ECONOMIC, SOCIAL, AND POLITICAL ISSUES

Praeger Publishers New York London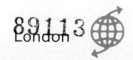

Library of Congress Cataloging in Publication Data

Main entry under title:

Youth crime and juvenile justice.

   (Praeger special studies in U.S. economic, social,
and political issues)
   Includes bibliographical references.
   1. Juvenile justice, Administration of—Addresses,
essays, lectures.   2. Deviant behavior—Labeling
theory—Addresses, essays, lectures.   3. Juvenile
delinquency—Prevention—Addresses, essays, lectures.
I. Friday, Paul C.   II. Stewart, V. Lorne.
HV9069.Y63   1977   364   77-7820
ISBN 0-03-022646-5

PRAEGER SPECIAL STUDIES
200 Park Avenue, New York, N.Y., 10017, U.S.A.

Published in the United States of America in 1977
by Praeger Publishers,
A Division of Holt, Rinehart and Winston, CBS, Inc.

789   038   987654321

Printed in the United States of America

In November 1975 the American Society of Criminology held its annual meeting in Toronto, Ontario, Canada. The theme of the conference was "International Perspectives of Criminology," and scholars from Europe, the Middle East, Asia, Latin America, and North America gathered to present papers and exchange views on crime, delinquency, deviant behavior, and corrections.

This volume is a selection of papers that were delivered at the Toronto meeting, whose program chairman was Arnold Trebach. It is one of a series of books coming out of that meeting.

For the record, the officers of the American Society of Criminology at the time of the Toronto meeting were:

President: Nicholas N. Kittrie, the American University;
President-Elect: Gilbert Geis, University of California at Irvine;
Vice-President: Paul C. Friday, Western Michigan University;
Vice-President: Terrence P. Thornberry, University of Pennsylvania;
Secretary: Barbara R. Prince, Pennsylvania State University; and
Treasurer: Harry E. Allen, the Ohio State University.

LIST OF TABLES AND FIGURES

Youth Crime and Juvenile Justice

1

INTERNATIONAL PERSPECTIVES ON JUVENILE JUSTICE AND YOUTH CRIME

Paul C. Friday
V. Lorne Stewart

The phenomenon of youth deviating from cultural and social norms is ubiquitous. Each generation perceives the next as more deviant and criminally prone. It is not clear if the phenomenon has changed or if our perceptions have changed, but youth crime and delinquency continue to occupy a place of concern—and debate—about social policies regarding it.

While assumptions and responses may vary on the subject, there is some international consistency. Youth crimes appear to be more frequent, and serious, in urban, industrial, affluent societies. The offenses perpetrated are generally against property and committed by younger males—although female youth offenses are increasing. Such data are reflected in both official and hidden delinquency figures.

In this volume we have assembled a number of studies dealing with juvenile justice and youth crime in industrialized, affluent societies. The first three studies describe the systems in Argentina, the United States, and England and Scotland. These three localities represent a range of responses from the purely legalistic definitions of violations of the penal code in Argentina to a nonlegalistic, highly social welfare component in Scotland. The studies are not analytical, but descriptive. They do, however raise a basic issue of policy. As Paul Nejelski asks in the U.S. study, is the juvenile court to be a court or a social agency?

Each author seems discontented with the elements of his own system—the selection of differentials in Argentina, the philosophy of state intervention and indeterminate sentences in the United States, and the futility of using the juvenile court as an extension of community

---

The editors would like to acknowledge the competent assistance in editing by Carolyn Fike.

welfare services in England. But does the failure lie in the structure of the procedures or more in the dynamics of the social conditions surrounding the behavior?

The chapters following the descriptions of juvenile court structures attempt to look more closely at the effects of current policy
and thereby draw some conclusions regarding the future direction
policy should take, as well as provide some clues to the dynamics
surrounding the act and adjudication.

The chapter by Christopher Sieverdes and Clemens Bartollas
looks at the modes of adaptation and game behavior at two juvenile
institutions. They typologize the adaptations into Robert Merton's
types: conformist, innovator, ritualist, retreatist, and rebel. They
argue that juvenile institutions are not unlike adult correctional facilities; they are cruel, brutal, and violent. They suggest that the
modes of adaptation can be matched by age, sex, race, body size and
structure, prior institutionalization, and inmate pecking order.

By looking more closely at the adaptations, greater knowledge
can be gained regarding the ultimate effectiveness of possible treatment modalities for certain types of juveniles. Clearly, the future
of juvenile institutions is uncertain. Pressures are being exerted
both to increase as well as decrease their use. Sieverdes and Bartollas provide some basis for measuring the possible impact of institutionalization.

The issue of the impact of official responses to youth crime has
been of concern for many years. Much of this concern has focused
less on the institution itself and more on the subsequent chances of
the offender adopting conforming behavior. In general, effectiveness
has been measured in terms of recidivism, and recidivism has been
viewed as a function of the negative consequences of officially labeling
an offender "delinquent."

The dilemma faced by the U.S. juvenile system—whether to act
as a court or as a social agency—revolves around the issue of labeling.
Does labeling ultimately lead to a negative self-concept, secondary
deviance, and subsequently reinvolvement in crime? The chapters
by Charles W. Thomas and Gideon Fishman both challenge the deter-
minism of labeling theory. The authors, coming from different orientations, view the process of responding to the label by recidivating
as much more complex than traditional thinking.

Thomas seeks to predict recidivism on the basis of official court
data and offers some interesting insights into the predictability of
general social background and offense characteristics. He carefully
and methodically analyzes and evaluates the predictive value of each
variable included in official records. His multivariate analysis suggests that a new interpretation is necessary for the variables traditionally used for prediction: school attendance, race, sex, and socioeconomic status.

Fishman likewise argues that labeling does not automatically lead to recidivism. He attempts to redefine the impact of the adjudication process and the experiences of youth in a delinquency treatment center. He argues that recognition of the label by the delinquent might indicate a greater awareness of expected behavior and symbolize a greater acceptance of the community's social control function. Fishman is concerned with the sensitivity of the offender to others' expectations and argues for policy geared toward determining "good risks."

Thus, Thomas argues for greater longitudinal studies that measure the impact of influences not recorded in official data, and Fishman suggests such an influence is the acceptance or rejection of the deviant label. In many respects, the three chapters dealing with institutionalization of juveniles reflect the query posed by Nejelski in his paper, "How Do You Know Where You're Going If You Don't Know Where You Are?"

The answer is not simple by any means, but the remaining chapters in this volume attempt, in one way or another, to deal with the basic, fundamental issues surrounding the involvement of youth in criminal activity. All try to provide a clue to a better understanding of the dynamics of delinquency. All try to isolate the variables affecting initial involvement, judicial selection, and adaptations to labeling.

The theme of the remaining chapters is social integration; the variables mitigating for or against it. Social integration implies commitments to conformity, the acceptance of informal social controls, close ties with significant others, and the adoption of general societal value patterns. Depending on the degree, social integration could serve as a prophylaxis against crime, provide a frame of reference for viewing the juvenile courts' role—court or social agency—determine institutional modes of adaptation, or sensitize one to the application of the delinquent label.

Juvenile justice and youth crime need to be viewed within the total context of social integration both in demographic and individual terms. The chapters by Josine Junger-Tas and David Shichor and Alan Kirschenbaum look at the extent of youth crime in Belgium and Israel, drawing implications for this theoretical model and juvenile justice policy.

Junger-Tas's hidden delinquency study supported the theoretical assumptions of theories stressing social integration and the importance of positive and meaningful experiences at home, school, or work. Such positive experiences were seen as integrative, tending toward greater conformity.

Shichor and Kirschenbaum rely on official records in discussing the extent and depth of delinquency in Israeli development (new) towns.

Using official records of socioeconomic indicators, they reveal several significant relationships between unemployment, overcrowding in schools, homogeneity and age of the community, distance of the new town from more established communities, and the like. Perhaps the strongest variables related to recidivism in the Shichor and Kirschenbaum study were unemployment and quality of education—both factors related to social integration and the development of commitment to conformity.

Paul Friday and John Halsey attempt to define the processes by which social integration is facilitated—positive family, school, community, work, or peer relationships. They argue that if youth have intimate role relationships in all five areas and a greater degree of overlap of these roles between the various groups, the probability of involvement in criminality will decrease. But it is a matter of degree and extent to which each group is able to play the integrative role that determines this outcome.

Two chapters, Leo Davids' and Giora Shoham's et al., deal with family relationships; those by Friday and Halsey and Peter Kratcoski and John Kratcoski deal with the schools; Joseph Fitzpatrick looks at the impact of community involvement. Each study draws its own policy implications, yet they all follow the same theme—positive relations in the home, school, community, or work is the best crime prevention policy.

Davids emphasizes the need for the development of positive relations with the father, an often neglected source of socialization. He stresses the need for courts to pay more attention to the role played by fathers and urges policy directed at improving that parent's role.

Shoham et al. take a psychiatric view of family relations utilizing much of the early assumptions about the individual's early relations with his mother. Employing a methodology that seeks to distinguish between the schizophrenic and delinquent, the authors conclude that the etiology of the two is similar, resting on a breakdown of interaction during the socialization process—particularly during the postoral stage of self-concept (ego boundary) development. The authors conclude the common denominator between schizophrenia and delinquency is a skewed family situation, but the difference lies in the delinquent's sensitivity to conflicts on "content" and the schizophrenic's sensitivity to "tone."

Friday and Halsey, after reviewing the theoretical support for the social integration hypothesis, elaborate on ways in which the school can assume some of the social service functions required by the courts. In essence, they argue for a redefinition and reutilization of schools, for less alienation and competition, the elimination of tracking, and the development of a community consciousness through

the school. Their assumption is that schools should facilitate greater
overlap of role relationships, thus providing more opportunities for
social integration.

Kratcoski and Kratcoski emphasize another dimension of social
integration—the impact and effectiveness of peers in the school setting.
Employing scales to measure socioeconomic status and self-reported
delinquency, they evaluate the effects of the dominant social class
of the school and the individual's own status. They emphasize the
importance of the context of social interaction, the atmosphere and
climate of the school, and how these affect both value orientations and
behavior.

In the final chapter, Fitzpatrick looks at the role of community
action projects in the prevention and treatment of youth crime. The
Youth and Community Alerted Project (JYCA) in Puerto Rico was
based on the theory that the development of community competence
and responsibility was an effective preventor and corrector of delinquent behavior. Essentially, the community was seen to replace the
juvenile court as a means of dealing with troubled youth. Community
members assumed responsibility often given to authorities—sanction-
ing their deviant young. Such an assumption of responsibility actually
facilitated integration and demonstrated the positive use of labeling
as Fishman discussed it.

The thrust of this book, then, is to look at the varying perspectives of scholars from North and South America, Europe, and the
Middle East. There is amazing consensus regarding the lack of
effectiveness of current systems. By probing deeper into the dynamics of youth interaction and response patterns a clearer picture emerges for future policy.

Policy makers need to reorient themselves into thinking about
the total interaction pattern of the offender—home, school, work,
community, and peer. The universal objective in juvenile justice is
to do what is in the best interest of both the youth and the community;
to do so requires, therefore, greater awareness of the source of
weakened commitments and attempts to build upon these areas of
integration previously ignored.

A society cannot deal with delinquency out of context; it cannot
evaluate the effectiveness or ineffectiveness of its courts or corrections without understanding the role they play in the development of
commitments to conformity. Efforts need to be made on all levels
to increase integration, whether those efforts come from the home,
school, community, courts, or detention centers. If these efforts
are not made, we are destined to continue our current pattern of
failure.

2

JUVENILE JUSTICE
IN ARGENTINA
Pedro R. David

There are two perspectives for defining juvenile delinquency in the Argentine legal system. The first is defined strictly by the Argentine Penal Code. It includes acts that are defined as crimes for both juveniles and adults. It is composed of major offenses such as robbery, theft, and rape. Regarding the second, there are a wide variety of acts such as drunkenness and disorderly conduct that are not included in the penal code but are included in the "Codes of Contraventions." The "Codes of Contraventions" define acts that are less serious than those in the penal code. Thus, the individual does not have to pass through a courtbound judicial process. While major penal crimes are adjudicated by means of a court-based judicial process that ultimately ends with a decision by a judge, contraventions are "cleared" by the municipal chief of police himself. The chief of police can either issue penalties of up to 30 days in jail, or he can do nothing. The penal code is uniform for the whole nation, but contraventions are specific state and municipal edicts or laws. Therefore, in Argentina, the cases processed by the juvenile courts represent only violations of the penal code, not violations of contraventions. The latter type cases are sometimes available in a police file but, if available, they are unreliable because of the informally cleared cases.

The Argentine Penal Code Law 14.394 specifies three categories of youth that may be subject to juvenile court disposition when they violate the criminal statutes:

1. less than 16 years of age;
2. 16 to 18 years of age;
3. 18 to 22 years of age.

Children less than 16 years of age cannot be held legally responsible for their criminal acts. They can be taken under the protection
of the court and committed to an institution for the protection of minors
if the juvenile court finds that either their personalities, family conditions, or general environments warrant such a disposition. They
go through no formally defined hearing or trial.

Children 16 to 18 years of age are responsible for their acts.
If they commit a crime that would result in a year or less in jail,
they are still not subject to the regular criminal judicial process.
If they commit a crime that would result in a year or more in jail,
they are subject to the criminal judicial process even though the
regular criminal penalties for adults are not applied. In these cases,
too, the judge can probate the children or commit them to special
institutions for the protection of minors. The chief difference between these children and those under 16 years of age is that the former are not judicially processed, but some of these may be.

Those 18 to 22 years of age are considered mentally responsible
and are subject to the criminal judicial process and its full range of
penalties. The penalties are, however, served in special institutions
for youths, away from older criminals.

The Argentine legal process places great weight on police evidence and police testimony. For most cases, what the police can
establish as the "legal truth" will generally become judicially confirmed. They are not likely to detain a citizen on a nebulous charge.
In addition, there is no plea bargaining in the Argentine system. The
police arrest a citizen when they can establish participation in or commission of a crime; the defendant's willingness to plead guilty or to
deny guilt is of little consequence; there must be a trial in any event.
Occasionally, when the police lack evidence to fix a more serious
degree of criminality they, too, will change the charge to a lesser
inclusive offense. However, systematic and regular changes in charges
from the time of booking to the time of judicial disposition do not
regularly occur, except occasionally when an influential family is
involved.

In other ways the official juvenile court statistics in Argentina
overrepresent certain sectors: the poor, the undereducated, the
legally unrepresented, the unstable families. While members of
these sectors might commit more delinquent acts, one thing is certain: status factors influence the official recording and adjudication
of delinquent children. The system operates in ways to favor the
children of the affluent. A case in point is one in which the appearance in court of parents or teachers before the police or the judge
gives evidence of better future vigilance and better future supervision. Such appearances stress the more positive resources for
correcting the children's behavior and inclines the judge to render

more favorable decisions to such children. By contrast, the orphaned or the abandoned or undefended children of the poor, for the lack of this appearance, have less opportunity to avoid incarceration or official records as delinquents; thus a class bias occurs in the official statistics.

Alternatives to imprisonment of minors in separate but essentially similar jails to those used for adults became generally available to Argentine federal judges as well as to those in provincial courts in 1919. Article 14 of Law Nacional 10.093 provides:

> Judges in the Capital of the Republic and in the provinces or national territories who have criminal and correctional jurisdiction before whom appears a person of less than 18 years of age accused of or as a victim of a crime shall, as a preventive measure, commit that minor to the National Council for Minors or adopt such other precautionary measures as the law allows if the minor is found to be materially or morally abandoned or in moral danger. In such cases, the legal provisions for preventive detention shall not be available in the ordinary federal courts of the Federal Capital and in the national territories. Preventive detention shall only be decreed when the judge considers it necessary, and shall be served only in an establishment of the National Council for Minors. It shall also be possible for the judge to leave the minor with his parents, guardian, or other responsible person under the general supervision of the National Council for Minors.

The same statute goes on to provide in Article 15:

> The same judges, when they dismiss a case against a person of less than 18 years of age either provisionally or finally or when they absolve such a person or when they definitely resolve a case in which such a person has been a victim of a crime, shall be able to commit the person for an indeterminate period up to 21 years of age in the same way established in the previous article if he is found to be materially or morally abandoned or in moral danger.

Moral and material abandonment or moral danger are defined by the statute to include urging of the minor by the parents (guardian or other responsible person) to commit acts prejudicial to his physical or moral health, begging or vagrancy, frequenting immoral or gambling places, and keeping company with thieves or vicious or ill-re-

puted persons. It is also moral danger for a minor under 18 years
of age to sell magazines or books or objects of any nature on the
streets or in public places, to work in such places without the supervision of his parent or guardian, or to work at any job prejudicial to
his health or morals.

Included in the statute is a requirement that the executive branch
of the federal government present a general plan for the construction
of special facilities for juveniles in the capital, in the national terri-
tories, and in the provinces. Included are schools for those found
abandoned or in danger, detention homes for those with behavior problems or for those who have violated the law, and reformatories for
the more dangerous.

The National Criminal Court of Appeals of Buenos Aires, a
High Tribunal composed of 18 judges, has been empowered by law
10.903 and in accordance with rulings of the court, to appoint three
judges who shall have the responsibility of supervising the treatment
and the policies given to delinquent or abandoned minors under 18 in
the Federal District of Buenos Aires and in all federal institutions in
the nation. I am one of the three. We are elected annually and can
be reelected.

Among our serious concerns is the situation posed by old build-
ings that after more than 50 years no longer meet the needs for adequate treatment of youth. Nor are we less concerned with the need
to upgrade the technical capabilities of administrative and judicial
staff.

We have assured cooperation and permanent dialogue with the
many organizations, public and private, concerned with the problem;
the National Ministry of Social Welfare, the Federal Police, the Ministry of Justice, the Ministry of Education, local governments, and
private agencies.

This regimen for the protection of minors in Argentina is crit-
icized on a number of counts. The lack of a system of specialized
courts for minors is alleged to restrict the development of an efficient,
prompt, and well-informed judicial response to situations of minors
in trouble. All the deficiencies of the Argentine criminal justice system for adults are alleged to pervade juvenile cases as well for this
reason. Argentine institutions for the treatment and correction of
minors at both the federal and provincial level are labeled as plainly
inadequate—as schools for graduation into more serious crime. Technical difficulties attributable largely to inadequate financial support
are cited as the reasons why these institutions fall short of the purposes for which they were created. It is alleged that, in many cases,
the operating personnel lack the technical training required for the
role they perform, a condition at least partially explained by the low
salaries offered. The greatest problem, however, is alleged to be

an overcrowding that far exceeds the efficient operating capacity of the institutions.

The challenge is formidable and the resources few, but I see a very distinct trend toward improvement.

3

JUVENILE JUSTICE IN
THE UNITED STATES
Paul Nejelski

Although approximately half the crime in the United States is committed by juveniles, juvenile courts traditionally have been relegated to a second-class status and generally forgotten by the lawyers, legislators, and planners. As one judge rather ineloquently commented, "The juvenile court in the United States is the latrine duty of the judiciary. You put in a few years and hope you will be promoted to a more prestigious court paying better with fewer problems."

It is, of course, paradoxical that the work of the juvenile court is at least as important as the general trial courts. The people who appear in juvenile and family courts have enormous problems. These courts are society's last resort in attempting to deal with the breakdown of families, cultural traditions, and other related social institutions such as schools.

A recent survey of conditions in the United States noted the following signs of disintegration in the family:

1. For the first time a majority of U.S. mothers hold jobs outside the home;
2. There is one divorce for every two marriages;
3. Teenage drug and alcohol abuse continues to rise;
4. A second leading cause of death among young Americans between 15 to 24 is suicide;
5. Every year, 1 million children run away from home, and this figure represents mainly middle-class children (there are many more children who leave home and simply move in with an older brother, other family member, or friend and are never reported to the police or other authorities);
6. A social psychiatrist recently concluded that the middle class today is approaching a level of social disorganization that

traditionally characterized low-income families of the early 1960s,
particularly as it is reflected in broken homes, working mothers,
and child abuse.

In addition to the breakdown in family and cultural traditions,
we are also confronted with a fiscal crisis in the state governments.
New York City is not alone in its difficulty in providing minimal social
services to its population. It is doubtful that significant increases in
resources will be available for prevention, diversion, or court processing of juveniles. One corollary is a growing understanding in
the United States that we cannot justify massive intervention in the
life of a juvenile and family based on the hope that in the future there
will be more resources, more programs, more group homes, or
more psychiatric counseling.

Prior to 1968, the juvenile court had been largely forgotten by
the courts, legal scholars, and lawyers in general. Although the
first juvenile court was founded in 1899 in Chicago, the first United
States Supreme Court review did not occur until almost 70 years later
with the celebrated Gault decision in 1967. Gault held that under the
federal contribution there was (1) a right to counsel, (2) a right to
confront and cross-examine witness, (3) a right to notice of charges,
and (4) a right to remain silent in the juvenile court. Although the
implementation of Gault and the rights enunciated therein has been
uneven in the United States, there has been an increase in the number
of lawyers appearing both as defense counsel and representatives of
the state. There has been greater pressure that the juvenile court
judge be a lawyer, and there has been a trend to greater use of tran-
scripts and appellate review.

But Gault and the subsequent Supreme Court cases have not
necessarily been a panacea. They have instead underlined the question of whether the juvenile court is a court or a social agency. The
U.S. legal scholar Roscoe Pound had special interest in the juvenile
court, and two statements of his emphasized the tensions between
the court and the role of the social agency. Early in the history of
the juvenile court movement, Pound said that the juvenile court was
the greatest innovation since the Magna Carta—obviously an enthu-
siastic endorsement of the court, but not unrealistic in light of the
fact that it has pioneered many of the institutions and practices
thought to be reforms in the early part of the century—probation,
the use of social history in sentencing, indeterminate sentences, and
even preventive detention. Writing approximately 20 years later,
Pound took a more sober view of the juvenile court when he said
that the court had the greatest power since the infamous Star chamber
of seventeenth century England. Needless to say, until Gault the juvenile judge largely had unbridled power. Frequently, with no counsel
present for either side, informality prevailed.

It is important to note that, while the juvenile justice system is growing in many ways similar to the adult adversarial system, the latter over the years has grown to be more like the juvenile system. For example, presentence reports, probation, and indeterminate sentences have all been introduced for better or worse into the adult system. In many respects the two are growing together—each progressing toward a middle ground rather than either being coopted by the other.

Despite the similarity between the two systems, there will always be special problems in any court that deals with juveniles because of the status of young people in our society. For example, there are problems of separating the interests of parents from those of the children. In many cases, not only should the child have counsel but the parent's separate interest should also be represented. Too often in the past the parent has been willing to waive the rights of their children with hopes of reaching a quick disposition. Then, too, children are always in someone's custody, whether it is the parent, the school, or juvenile court. In addition, their immaturity, reflected by their inability to write letters or otherwise make their plight known, creates special problems when they are incarcerated or have run away from home.

In many ways it is easier for experts from abroad to discuss conditions in their countries since they are often governed by a single statute that has application throughout the country. In contrast, the United States includes the 50 states, the District of Columbia, and the federal regulation, all of which make it very difficult to generalize about the state of juvenile justice in the United States.

Several areas that have been of growing concern in the wake of Gault should be pointed out. Before reviewing those areas, however, I would like to emphasize that it is useful not only to look at juvenile cases and problems by themselves but also to remember that they are part of a growing revolution in American thinking and the law about treatment of the mentally ill, about victimless crime, and about welfare and poverty law.

For instance, "Persons in Need of Supervision" (PINS) statutes establish juvenile court jurisdiction over such behavior as being beyond the control of parents. Are such laws void for vagueness? Here we might look to analogies in the vagrancy laws, which have been successfully attacked in the United States for too broad a delegation of power to the arresting and sentencing authorities.

COERCION—LIMITS ON STATE INTERVENTION

Judges, lawyers, legal scholars, legislators, and others concerned about children are becoming more cautious about the amount

of intervention in the lives of families and children. Research has
suggested that there is a higher rate of recidivism for those "treated"
by the courts and institutions than those who simply go their own way.
In addition, provision of some of these services is extremely expensive. Jerry Miller and his program to deinstitutionalize the Massachusetts treatment-correctional system a few years ago won a great
deal of support by pointing out that the cost of incarceration of a juvenile at that time was approximately $10,000, a sum that would buy a
college education, psychiatric treatment, and even a trip to Europe.
Instead, children were placed in regimented and unimaginative institutions, which were, in many cases, little more than holding camps
designed to keep kids off the street.

We are evolving toward a notion of "crisis intervention"—intervene only if there is a specific problem that the state can help resolve.
Avoid long-term "treatment." Models here include providing immediate services for runaways and the Sacramento Diversion Project,
which has been sponsored by the Davis Center for Criminal Justice
under the direction of Floyd Feeney. In this latter type of program
rapid intervention is made at juvenile court intake in an attempt to reduce pretrial incarceration, and even the necessity for a hearing itself.

PROPORTIONALITY

Should a shoplifter or truant spend the same amount of time in
correctional institutions as the armed robber or murderer? Some
are concerned that the indeterminate sentence lacks elements of essential fairness. In addition, statistics indicate that the status offenders,
such as children beyond the control of their parents, spend longer
time in institutions than those who have committed an offense that
would be a crime if they were adults. Often status offense children
come from a situation where there is little or no home. Disenchant-
ment with the indeterminate sentence for adults is making itself felt.
There is a notion that the time spent in an institution—whether under
the rationale of retribution, punishment, social defense, or some
other—should be in some way related to the offense. An analogy here
can be seen in the field of mental illness where there is a growing
sentiment that it is not fair to lock up someone until he is "treated."

TRANSFER OR WAIVER TO ADULT COURT

In most jurisdictions except New York, it is possible to transfer serious offenses to be tried into the normal criminal court in the

state. The alternative is the one adopted by New York, a relatively low age (15) for the ceiling of the jurisdiction of the juvenile court, with no transfer for even serious crimes such as murder. Society is becoming increasingly concerned about serious offenses being committed by juveniles. In New York there is evidence that juveniles are being used to carry narcotics or even used as "trigger men" for execution in gang wars. There is a serious pressure to increase the number of transfers or to introduce them into New York, which has none at the moment. The defenders of a restrictive transfer system point out that minority children—blacks, Puerto Ricans, Chicanos— are disproportionately subject to transfer to adult court.

THE SCOPE OF DUE PROCESS

The United States Supreme Court in the Kent decision in 1966, interpreting the District of Columbia transfer statute, found that some decisions about the disposition of children are so important as to require "ceremony," and that transfer to an adult court was one of these decisions. Consequently, the Supreme Court found that a hearing, right to counsel, a record that could be used by a reviewing court, and written reasons would be required in transfer proceedings under the District of Columbia statute. Many states adopted these principles in their own transfer proceedings.

However, the Richard Nixon administration cut back this grant of due process, and the District of Columbia obtained a federal statute that made transfer a matter of prosecutorial discretion. If certain crimes were charged (but not necessarily later proven) by the prosecutor, the case was to be automatically transferred to the adult criminal court. The United States Court of Appeals for the District of Columbia Circuit narrowly upheld this statute and invited Supreme Court review.

The Supreme Court declined this review (with three justices dissenting), and their comments may be prophetic. Among the issues on which the dissenters would have liked to have heard arguments was the question of whether or not the Administrative Procedure Act would apply to prosecutorial discretion. In looking to the future it is not inconceivable that intake decisions and decisions to release people from treatment-corrections programs, as well as prosecutorial discretions in transfer, may be subjected to at least some of the formality of administrative law, such as written administrative decisions and court review.

I should like to conclude my remarks by emphasizing the need to study the impact of these standards or any other changes in the juvenile justice system. Unfortunately, we are only at the beginning of achieving the necessary experience and data to measure what is really happening in the juvenile justice system. Record keeping has been lamentable throughout the system.

If we and our institutions are to survive, we must of necessity become an experimenting society. We must test diversion as Frank Zimring of the University of Chicago has done so skillfully in his study of the Vera Manhattan Court employment project or test the effects of deinstitutionalization in Massachusetts as the Harvard Center for Criminal Justice under Jim Vorenberg and Lloyd Olin has attempted. We must begin by collecting the necessary base line data and, where possible, assign rigid control group experiments.

In sum, we must remove the level of discourse from one of theological dispute about the merits of alternative strategies and attempt to measure the impact of current and proposed programs. It is impossible to devise a strategy for transfer to adult court when we do not know how many children are transferred to adult court, for what types of offenses, for how long, whether they are later convicted, and what the disposition is in adult criminal court.

I have already set forth many of my views on this subject in an article, "Monitoring the Juvenile Justice System: How Do You Know Where You're Going If You Don't Know Where You Are?" (1974). Rather than continue in this vein, I would close with a final word taken from Roscoe Pound: "It is a good thing for lawyers and social workers to be suspicious of each other." Both professions have strengths; both have weaknesses. In the United States there should and would be a general suspicion of a system where either reigned supreme.

REFERENCE

Nejelski, Paul. 1974. "Monitoring the Juvenile Justice System: How Do You Know Where You're Going If You Don't Know Where You Are?" American Criminal Law Review 12:9-31.

4

JUVENILE JUSTICE IN ENGLAND AND SCOTLAND
John M. Gandy

Just as there are important differences in criminal law and procedure between England and Scotland, so there are equally important differences in social conditions and culture that are reflected in both policy and procedures in the juvenile justice system. For instance, in 1969 when legislation was passed creating the present juvenile justice system in Scotland, only 16 percent of the cases involving juveniles were heard in specially constituted juvenile courts. England, on the other hand, pioneered in the development of juvenile courts using lay magistrates.

ENGLAND

The Children's and Young Persons Act (1969) raised the age of criminal responsibility in England from 10 to 12 years and instituted a number of changes in the juvenile justice system that were designed to substitute treatment for punishment. To this end, a child under the age of 12 may be proceeded against only by "care" proceedings, and the commission of an offense is only one of the factors to be taken into account in deciding whether a "care" order should be made. The intent of that change was to abolish, for young children, the distinction between the deprived child and the deliberately offending child. However, any social worker, police constable, or an officer of the National Society for the Prevention of Cruelty to Children (NSPCC) can bring a child under the age of 17 years to the juvenile court if that person has "reason to believe (the child) is in need of care and control." A child in need of care and control is one who is beyond the control of his parents, exposed to moral danger, truanting, dependent or neglected, or who has committed an offense (excluding homicide).

If the child is committed to the care of the local social work department, that department has legal custody until the child is 18 years of age (or 19, under special conditions); social workers decide to which type of residential accommodation to send the offender, or whether to allow him to remain at home. The proceedings in the English juvenile courts are conducted before one to three magistrates, who are drawn from a panel with the provision that one of the panel members will be a woman. The court may issue an order committing the child to the care of the local social work department, order his parents to exercise proper guardianship, make a supervision order (formerly a Probation Order), or issue a hospital or guardianship order under the Mental Health Act. Supervision may include conditions regarding treatment or participation in noncustodial community programs. The English juvenile court has the following dispositional alternatives, in addition to those mentioned above, with respect to care proceedings: fines up to 50 pounds (about $100), compensation to the victim, order an offender to attend an "attendance center," detention in a detention center (a short-term correctional institution for up to six months), commit for Borstal training, conditional discharge, or an absolute discharge. A juvenile between the ages of 12 and 17 who is charged with an offense may also be subject to criminal proceedings if the juvenile is charged jointly with an adult. If he is found guilty and not discharged or fined, he is sent to the juvenile court for disposition.

An important change in the English system came with the passage of the 1969 act, when magistrates lost the power to (1) decide what should be done with a child's "care" and (2) send juveniles to approved schools (training schools). Some critics have claimed that this has resulted in more commitments of 15- to 17-year-olds to detention centers and Borstals, which were designed to serve small groups of persistent and "hard core" youthful offenders. From 1969 to 1973 there was an increase of 67 percent in sentences that involved periods in detention centers; the comparable figure for Borstals was about 50 percent.

The most recent change in the English juvenile justice system has given social work departments major responsibility for one of ten juveniles seen in courts. The intent was to make the system more flexible, but there has been widespread criticism because of the lack of community services. One result is that magistrates are having to remand young people to adult prisons and remand centers because of the lack of secure places in the community. The number of 14- to 16-year-olds on remand in prisons and remand centers has increased from under 3,000 in 1971 to more than 4,600 in 1974. There is also a waiting period of up to six weeks for children to gain admission to an assessment center. A related criticism is that the loss of

control by the court over juveniles in care of social work departments
has resulted in an increase in juvenile crime. The magistrates are
particularly concerned that they have no sanctions if a juvenile does
not pay a fine or if he breaches a supervision order.

England represents a prime example of the futility of trying to
use the juvenile court as a simultaneous extension of the community's
social welfare services and the criminal justice system. Unlike the
situation in North America, the problem of providing legal safeguards
for juveniles has not been a major issue as changes in the system
have been introduced. In fact, the most recent changes in England appear to be moving the juvenile justice system in the direction of more
rather than less discretion in the handling of juvenile offenders.

SCOTLAND

When Scotland introduced major changes in its juvenile justice
system in 1969, it replaced its existing juvenile courts with a system
of "children's hearings" before a panel of lay persons. The result
has been a system with a higher social welfare component than that
of England. One of the major objectives was to create a structure in
which decision making regarding juvenile offenders would be placed
in the hands of as broad a cross section of the community as possible.
A related objective was to reduce the conflict between the procedure
of the criminal court and the claims regarding the welfare of the children. Although there were marked changes in the structure, there
were no changes in the age of criminal responsibility—it remains between 8 and 16 years.

Social workers, doctors, friends, neighbors, the child's parents, or the police may refer a child to a local official, appointed by
the secretary of state, who is known as a "reporter." Each local authority has such an appointed official, who has almost absolute discretion in carrying out his responsibilities as "gatekeeper" for the juvenile justice system. When the reporter receives an allegation from
one of the above sources he may choose to take no official action (that
is, instead he may write a letter to the parents), or he may suggest
to the parents that the child receive voluntary supervision from the
social worker. However, if he decides that compulsory action is required, a Children's Hearing is convened, which is provided with a
written statement of the facts of the case, to decide on the disposition
of the case.

A Children's Hearing is conducted by a panel of three members
of the community, one of whom must be a woman. Others present
must include the reporter (who has the responsibility for administer-
ing the hearings but does not participate as a member of the panel),

the child, and his parents. A representative from the local social
work department usually attends, but this is not mandatory; provision
is also made that a representative (usually a minister or family
friend) chosen by the child or his family may attend. Studies have
shown that the average time of the hearings is about 30 minutes.
The dispositions available to the panel include: a supervision requirement administered by the local social work department, a voluntary organization, or an individual and carried out in the community;
supervision with the requirement that the child be removed from his
home to a residential establishment; referral to an educational authority for assessment; referral to a mental health officer for consideration for admission to a hospital; and discharge with no further action.

One of the most important characteristics of the Scottish system
is the relationship of the panel to the criminal courts. There is a
clear division of responsibility between adjudication and the decision
concerning treatment. If the child and his parents accept the written
statement of the allegations sent to them by the reporter, the hearing can then proceed. If they do not, the case will go to the sheriff
(a criminal court judge) who will hear the evidence, determine the
facts of the case, and send the child back to the hearing for disposition if the allegations are proven to be true. Legal representation is
allowed in the sheriff's court, and legal aid may be granted.

The sheriff's court is also involved in the event of an appeal by
the child or his parents against a decision of the children's panel.
The child and/or his parents may then be legally represented before
the sheriff. There is also a further appeal to a higher court on a point
of law, or in respect of any irregularity in the conduct of the case.
This appeal from a decision of the sheriff may be initiated by the child,
his parent(s), or the reporter.

The third type of involvement of the sheriff's court occurs in the
case of certain serious offenses where the procurator fiscal prose-
cutes on the instruction of the lord advocate. Prosecution is also possible where technical considerations could prevent a Children's Panel
from dealing completely with a case, or where a child is charged
jointly with an adult. However, the sheriff's court may ask the panel
for a recommendation regarding disposition, but this is not binding.

Another important characteristic of the Scottish system is the
provision for a review by the panel of their earlier decision. Compulsory supervision has no fixed time limit, and children may remain
under the authority of the hearing until the age of 18. All supervision
requirements must be reviewed within one year, but, in addition to
this, there is provision that a review may be requested by the social
work department, the child, his parents or the reporters after three
months and thereafter at six intervals.

There have been criticisms that the lay panels do not represent
a cross section of the community. Some steps are being taken to

meet this criticism by more aggressive recruitment of young persons and persons of low income. As in England, there is criticism that the panels are too lenient on persistent offenders. Another frequent criticism, particularly by panel members, is that the needed community resources have not been provided, resulting in too many juveniles being sent to residential centers. Also, assessment centers have been forced to keep children for as long as three or four months before a place is found in an institution. Finally, many panel members feel that the dispositions available to them are too limited.

SUMMARY

In both countries recent changes have attempted to make the systems more flexible. Scotland has sought to involve the community in the process in a more meaningful manner. In England magistrates are selected for their knowledge of children and the system; hence, they represent a very select group of persons. On the other hand, in Scotland, persons are selected for the Children's Panels because of their knowledge of the community.

In both England and Scotland, despite recent changes, the juvenile justice systems are still related to the criminal justice process. However, in Scotland there has been more success in weakening the tie between the two systems and in achieving more informality, flexibility, and participation of youths and their families in the decision-making process. This is, indeed, an improvement; and, it is to be hoped that research currently under way will provide much needed factual data on this innovative juvenile justice system. It is clear, however, that in both countries insufficient resources have been provided for the implementation of the changes in the legislation. As a result, there has been continuous criticism from those who want more sanctions, as well as from those in the caring professions and pressure groups who maintain that the legislation is basically sound, but that it has been sabotaged by lack of resources.

5

MODES OF ADAPTATION AND GAME BEHAVIOR AT TWO JUVENILE INSTITUTIONS
Christopher M. Sieverdes
Clemens Bartollas

Various authors—Schrag (1954), Clemmer (1958), Sykes (1958), Giallombardo (1966), Irwin (1970), Heffernan (1972), and others—have pointed to the negative impact of correctional institutions on their residents. Beginning the day of entry into an institution and continuing throughout their stay, inmates are stripped of their previous community identity, are forced to interact with the "dregs of society," are denied many of their basic human rights, and are often exploited in all conceivable ways by other residents (Bartollas et al., 1975). They, in addition, are given the stigma of the "ex-con," which will go with them the rest of their days.

Inmates, not surprisingly, have devised several different ways to protect themselves against the degradation and the deprivations of this experience. According to Irwin, who served "time" in a California prison, prisoners pursue three different adaptational styles of institutional life (1970). One of these is "doing time" in which inmates pass through the prison experience with the least amount of trouble possible. "Jailing," another type of adaptation, is characterized by the inmate's attempts to maximize pleasures available in prison and gain prestige and power in the inmate society. The final type of adaptation is "gleaning"; in this reaction, the inmate tries to reform and use the prison milieu to make constructive changes in himself. Heffernan, in her description of "the square," "the cool," and "the life," portrayed in a similar way the reaction of incarcerated women to prison life (1972).*

---

*A much more developed typology of inmate adaptations to a correctional setting is found in Anne R. Edwards, "Inmate Adaptations and Socialization in the Prison," Sociology 4 (May 1970): 213-25.

Another popular mode of adaptation among inmates entails creation of an unwritten and informal code that protects them against the
staff's values and norms (Sykes and Messinger, 1960). Several authors have elaborated upon the normative code of inmates. McCorkle
and Korn, for instance, find that these conduct norms bolster the
residents' dignity and self-respect, while they promote solidarity and
cohesion (1962). Wellford, subsequently, has discovered that the
length of an inmate's sentence, the phase of his institutional career,
and his criminal social type are important factors related to the degree of inmate code adoption (1967). A number of other authors, however, have challenged the "solidarity opposition" of the inmate code
(Irwin and Cressey, 1962; Ward and Kassebaum, 1965; Giallombardo,
1966; Irwin, 1970; and Heffernan, 1972).

Inmates often rebel against the control of their captors and try
to take over control of the prison. They can do this through a major
disturbance, such as the riot at Attica, although the inevitable consequence of a riot is failure, humiliation, and perhaps injury or death.
A more productive consequence occurs when inmates bargain with
guards for institutional control and gain concessions as compensation
for conformity (McCleery, 1961a; McCleery, 1961b; Morris et al.,
1961). McCorkle, in this regard, points out that guards may be coopted and, thus, permit prisoners to do what they want (1962).

The juvenile institution, much as adult correctional facilities,
can be far more cruel and inhumane than most outsiders ever imagine
(Bartollas et al., 1976a). Even though some treatment institutions appear to have more trusting relationships with staff, less suspicion, and
more cooperation among residents (Street et al., 1966), it is more
common to find training schools in which residents are hostile to staff
and each other and determine their institutionalization to be a degrad-
ing experience (Barker and Adams, 1959; Fisher, 1961; Huffman,
1961; Polsky, 1962; Davis, 1968; and Bartollas et al., 1976b). Thus,
juveniles also must find ways to cope with their incarceration.

Bartollas et al. find from their study of a maximum security
male institution that residents tend to pursue one of the following
modes of adaptation: (1) pretend to internalize the values of staff; (2)
take on the hard line and confront staff at every turn; (3) play it "cool"
and "do one's time"; (4) try to make the present stay as pleasurable
as possible; and (5) withdraw either physically or emotionally (1976b). *
Residents, resenting the self-serving needs of staff, attempt to sur-

---

*These modes of adaptations are related closely to what is found
in Erving Goffman's Asylums (Garden City, N.Y.: Anchor Books,
1961). Goffman is describing how mental patients adapt to a "total institution."

vive in this particular institution by playing games with the staff
(Miller et al., 1975). The payoff from these games by participants
is manipulation of others to gain an advantage (Berne, 1964; 1972).*

Of major interest in the present statewide study of youth in
trouble are the effects of bureaucratic rules on incarcerated youth;
the quality of relationships among staff and residents; the quality of
relationships among inmates; the impact of coeducational training
schools on residents; and how different types of youth adapt to institutionalization. This particular paper compares the types of games
played by youngsters in two training schools as they attempt to deal
with their institutionalization.

METHODOLOGY

Sample Design

A sample of 263 juveniles was drawn from the populations of
two coeducational training schools in a southeastern state. The two
training schools had 138 and 148 students assigned to them at the
time of data collection. Twenty students from the former and three
from the latter were not included in the sample because of absence
from the institution, illness, and organization contingencies.

The survey questionnaires were administered and read to groups
of approximately 30 students by the authors. The residents answered
questions concerning their physical attributes, social and legal background, and 65 Likert scale questions. The Likert questions were concerned with the self-concept of students and their attitudes toward the
training school, staff members, and peers. In a secondary phase of
data collection, the residential staff in each of the student's cottages
were administered questionnaires designed to assess and classify
each of the students under their supervision with respect to his (or
her) attitude, methods of gaming and conning peers and staff members,
and the degree of dominance exerted over fellow inmates. The staff
members identified the nature of the cons or games that the juveniles

---

*Game behavior has been studied in other contexts. Kadushin
(1968) described how supervisees play games on supervisors. Ernst
and Keating, Jr. (1964) portrayed how felons in California prisons
play games in their therapy groups. Walker developed the games
that delinquents and their families play on their family counselor
(1974).

play in their social setting. Provided with a list of 19 games or modes
of behavior typically enacted within institutional settings, staff members selected those games that best characterized each of the juveniles.

The 19 games are compiled and collapsed into Merton's five
modes of adaptation (1938).* This study's conceptual model involves
identification of the different juvenile's modes of adaptation to institutional life. The Spearman Rank Order Correlation (Rho) is utilized
to examine the extent of correlation between each of the five model
types of incarcerated juveniles and their physical, demographic, social, and legal attributes. This documents the visible and behavioral
characteristics for each juvenile type.

The Institutions

A T-Test was employed to determine similarities of samples
drawn from the two training schools. Training school A tends to have
a heavier concentration of juveniles over the age of 14, whereas
training school B contains juveniles from 10 to 14 and a half years
old. Training school A generally is considered to be the institution
within the state system that juveniles enter prior to being sent to the
state's maximum security training school. Half the juveniles at this
training school are recidivists within the system. On the other hand,
training school B has more youth incarcerated in a state institution
for the first time; this training school now is considered to be a "first-
stop" for undisciplined youth or status offenders.[†] This is not to suggest that juveniles in training school B are novices within the local
court system or that the length of their current stay is necessarily
shorter. They simply have been referred to a state training school
less often than those in training school A.[‡]

---

*Merton's typology is made up of conformity, innovation, ritual-
ism, retreatism, and rebellion. According to Merton, these are the
possible adaptations to the cultural goal (success) of our society and
the institutional means of attaining this goal. This typology has been
applied to a wide range of research topics with varying success (see
Cole and Zuckerman, 1964).

[†]Up until a few months before this study began, training school
B was reserved for older, aggressive girls. A number of problems
developed that required the girls either to be released, sent to the state
maximum security institution, or transferred to training school A.

[‡]After a short period of time in the diagnostic center (there are
two diagnostic centers, each serving half the state), the customary

There are few notable differences between the populations of the two training schools sampled. Age, physical size, grade, age at the time of the first court referral, and frequency of running from the institution are differential interinstitutional factors. Training school A tends to have older, larger, and more delinquent juveniles. The proportion in the number of previous referrals to training school also is higher at training school A, but the difference is not statistically significant. Other characteristics of the juveniles are strikingly similar.

ANALYSIS OF DATA

Modes of Adaptation

Institutionalized juveniles exercise different modes of adjustment to their closed social environment. Youthful offenders, who usually deny that they are any different than other adolescents remaining in the community, know that they must pursue behavioral patterns that are an effective means of coping with an alien setting. That is, the residents want a short stay while they attempt to maximize the living comforts of their present setting. To cope with their setting, incarcerated youths must cope with the pressures of the inmate subculture, rule-enforcing staff members, and the internal confusion that the degradation of this experience brings to the self. There is no question that the contradictory role expectations create internal havoc with many residents.

Each resident experiences conflicting role expectations from staff and peers. The resident is faced with constant peer pressure to resist staff values. Rejection awaits those who cooperate with the staff too much. They are also informed by the staff—either cooperate with me or have a long stay. The degradation and mortification of this experience must become assimilated in the self-concept.

Some youths decide to conform or even overconform to a set of staff-imposed expectations. Others engage in patterns of manipulation, denial, role playing, or even rebellion and aggression. Some play ritualistic games with peers or staff because of boredom, frustration, stress, or alienation. If we have sufficient social, legal, and demographic data, the roles played by these youths are reasonably predictable. Such factors as sex, race, age, physical size, type of

---

tracking for the "status offender" is to their first-of-the-line institution.

offense, and length of prior institutionalization, to name a few, influence the type of roles that juveniles play in coping with their alien
environments. The typology of juveniles identified in this study appears to be an operationalization of Merton's five modal forms of
adaptation. They are described in the following section.

The Conformist

The juveniles identified as conformists are characterized by
unique sets of behaviors and patterns of adjustment to institutional
life. As these behaviors are manifested, the institutional staff members judge the juveniles to be good or "straight." Being very expres-
sive in their effort to impress the staff with their positive, conventional attitude, inmates attempt to flatter the staff with comments
they feel will evoke a positive attitude toward them. They also attempt to impress staff members with the amount of "progress" they
have made in the program during their stay. They make certain that
staff are aware of their positive attitude by overtly obeying all regu-
lations, by displaying remorse for having engaged previously in delinquent or aberrant behavior, and by doing everything possible to en-
hance the possibility of an early release. These youths in trouble
try to convince the staff that they are not members of the "training
school gang" and, therefore, do not really belong in a training school.
The success of their efforts is demonstrated by their rapid passage
through the institutional merit system.

Because these residents attempt to set themselves apart from
other "inmates," they do not try to con other students very often
($r = .111$) (rho is identified by r), and generally they are unsuccessful in their few such attempts ($r = .070$). Peers recognize their desire to make a good impression on the staff; consequently, they are
not trusted by fellow residents and are alienated from the inmate subculture. They are likely to become labeled as a snitch by peers and
experience mutual distrust and fear within the institution. A possible
reason is that conformists direct most of their attention to staff in-
stead of peers. They attempt to con staff relatively more often ($r = .196$), with more success ($r = .165$), than their peers. Girls, although not particularly successful in convincing staff, direct most of
their efforts to convincing staff that they are conformists ($r = .404$).
The white girls characteristically aim to convince their peers that
they are oriented to the staff, thereby, insulating them to some degree
from the inmate subculture.

Interestingly enough, the conformists are not readily identified
as a "con" and "manipulator" by staff, for they view the conformists'
behavior as an effort to overconform to institutional expectations. In-

TABLE 5.1

Gaming Behavior by Modes of Adaptation (Rho)

Gaming Behavior	Conformist	Innovator	Ritualist	Retreatist	Rebel
Greater number attempts to con peers	.111*	.240*	.205*	.009	.394*
More successes in conning peers	.070	.216*	.152*	-.033	.374*
Greater number attempts to con staff	.196*	.210*	.297*	-.015	.408*
More successes in conning staff	.165*	.093	.260*	-.112*	.258*
More often conned by peers	-.025	.081	.071	.187*	.163*
Greater level of dominance	.061	.062	.038	-.068	.237*
More often identified as not playing con games	.190*	.163*	.208*	.148*	.185*

*Each Rho coefficient is significant at the .05 level.

Source: Compiled by the authors.

stead of perceiving these youths as trying to "use" them, staff members feel that they are exhibiting prosocial behavior and do not really belong in a training school. Staff, thus, make every attempt to protect them from predatory peers.

The physical attributes of these juveniles set them apart from the rest of the school population. Most of the conformists are white, male, and a minimum of 14 years old at the time of their first court appearance. They come from an intact and stable family comprising both natural parents, but they have been institutionalized on account of a serious delinquent offense—namely, a felony involving a person or property.

In summary, the conformists are relatively intelligent juveniles from white, conventional, blue-collar homes who do not possess extended histories of delinquent activity. It is unlikely that they will return to the training school following release. They do not become involved in con games to any great extent with peers or staff members and, in turn, are not conned very much by others. Their isolation from the subculture reduces heavy involvement in manipulative interaction.

The Innovator

The master manipulators within the institutional setting are the innovators. These youths, in fact, may not be aware of the degree to which they calculate and form their rituals or interaction with staff members and peers. Their life pattern has been one of gratification, hedonism, and deception. When they finally are "busted" and adjudicated to a training school, they usually view themselves as a "fox," meaning that they must be shrewd enough to figure out the best angle or the best way to accomplish a goal. Other than their behavior component, innovators' only unique social and physical characteristic is their male gender. Among the males, blacks are slightly more innovative than whites. On the other hand only those girls who have been incarcerated frequently and for a long period of time attempt manipulation of peers and staff. They experience little success, because the staff comes to expect the girls to manipulate and con them for favorable results. In sum, the innovators focus their attention on peers ($r = .240$) more than on staff ($r = .210$), with better results with the former ($r = .216$). For girls the cost is high, since they themselves frequently are conned and manipulated ($r = .575$).

Innovators direct their attention to both peers and staff. The games they play most often with staff include excessive complaining about unequal distribution of privileges and denial of responsibility for institutional rule violations. Although they attempt to con staff frequent-

ly, their success rate is low (r = .093) because staff have become
wise to them. Staff members perceive these inmates as average in
terms of social dominance within the institutional setting and see them
as occasionally being conned by peers.

In their relationships with peers, the innovators can read potential victims skillfully and usually know how best to "out-fox" them.
Their frequent attempts net them success quite often in this endeavor.
The most typical games of this type toward other inmates involve sexual manipulation, exploitation, and gratification. Property and material possessions also provide a major source of peer-oriented gaming. They define property holdings as a primary means of gaining
power and prestige.

                              The Ritualist

The ritualists are normally the juveniles institutionalized most
often. These youths have a long history of delinquent offenses, as
evidenced by their early age at the time of their first court appearance, the greater than average length of their current incarceration,
and the total length of time that they have lived in private and state
juvenile institutions. Behaviorally, they attempt to live in a way that
fits the image of a con or person "living on the state." Their insecurity is often displayed in behavior that garners them much desired attention. While they try to act tough, this behavior is clearly superficial. The basic means of coping with institutional life consist of seeking the attention of other peers, exaggerating their delinquent record,
and generally making themselves noticeable to staff.

These youths form an image of expected inmate behavior and
characteristics, and they act out within the institutional setting the role
expectation that they perceive as befitting that image. Behavioral alternatives include acting the role of "punk," "tough," or "con." They
can be innovative and, at times, even rebellious; but they quickly back
down from a confrontation once their desires are made known. With
the exception of the rebellious juvenile, this type is more likely to go
through the motions of conning peers (r = .205) and staff (r = .297).
Their success rate is considerably higher for staff cons (r = .260)
than peer-oriented ones (r = .152) because the staff is forced to pay
attention to their behavior. The ritualists' games are unimaginative,
and peers and staff soon learn "where they are coming from"; but
they receive attention by becoming a nuisance or aggravation to those
around them. The ritualists among the girls are the white, chronically
institutionalized juveniles. Male ritualists are those having spent the
longest time in state institutions.

Staff members report, however, that these juveniles are less
con- or game-oriented than any of the other social types identified in

this study. This may be interpreted several ways: (1) these youths
are totally institutionalized and act out a pattern of behavior that institutional life requires; (2) they are accustomed to manipulating staff
and peers in a system in which they have resided for years, and their
gaming often is undetected; or (3) when staff become aware how much
these youths need attention and approval, they become more accepting
of their game behavior.

There is no question that the ritualists feel comfortable with incarceration and sometimes are even reluctant to leave the institution.
They occasionally "mess up" right before release to postpone their
return to the community. One of their favorite tactics in postponing
release is to escape several days before release and then return vol-
untarily to the institution.

The Retreatist

Retreatists are identifiable readily within the institutional structure because of their young age, small stature, and their introverted
manner. They are normally white males having a longer than average institutional stay due to previous escapes from training school.
Staff refer to this type as a "rabbit," which obviously is related to
their frequent absconding from this and other institutions. Finding
life very difficult in confinement, the open setting of institutions in
this state represents a constant temptation to run away.

The retreatists are not trusted by other youths in the inmate
subculture and typically serve as scapegoats for them. This makes
them more withdrawn, afraid, and desperate; they seek isolation,
which is difficult to attain in a closed institutional setting. They frequently are exploited, both sexually and materially, by more aggressive peers. Top administrators in both training schools are acutely
aware of the political ramifications of a high runaway rate; therefore,
they direct middle management and line staff to maintain "eyeball
supervision" on these potential runners. As a consequence staff feel
resentment and alienation toward these youths. Retreatists are aware
that staff do not trust them; and they, in turn, feel that everybody is
against them—staff as well as peers.

Although they are not adept at conning others and their success
rate at conning staff falls below the other residents ($r = -.112$), they
are conned by fellow peers more frequently than any other type ($r = .187$). Virtually no gender-related differences exist, except that
more white females are retreatists than any other type within the in-
stitutional setting. These inmates, very unhappy about being institutionalized, are extremely reluctant to enter into the social life within
the institutional setting. Not surprisingly, they are more prone to

hurt themselves or to commit suicide than the other four types. They
are clearly the scapegoat and continue the types of interactions that
fulfill this role.

The Rebel

The labels—rebel, bruiser, troublemaker, tough, and heavy—
apply to youths who physically control the inmate subculture through
coercion. In a racially integrated system, these juveniles are usually
an urbanized, older, black male who predominates in the social hierarchy of the cottage. Among the males, blacks and offense recidivists
tend to assert themselves as "bruisers." The chief characteristics
of their female counterparts are greater frequency and length of incarceration.

Staff consistently rank the rebels in the top third of the cottage
in terms of dominance. They are the most overtly active and successful game players in the institutional setting, for they attempt to con
students more than any other social type ($r = .394$) and have the highest success rate ($r = .374$). They also attempt to con the staff more
often than the other residents ($r = .408$) and enjoy a success rate as
high as that of ritualists ($r = .258$). In the close physical settings
of institutional life, every youth is aware of the presence of the
"bruiser."

Whenever changes occur in the inmate population, power struggles are common among the various physically dominant black males.*
Both institutions contain separate black and white inmate power structures. White bruisers dominate the majority of the white inmates;
black bruisers tend to dominate the entire population but do respect,
to some degree, the domain of the white bruisers.

Much of the rebels' interaction is directed toward the staff.
This type is quick to threaten and harass staff members, needling
them when they are tired or ill and playing one staff member off
against another. They spend most of their time testing limits imposed
by peers and supervisors, and they reject many of the conventional
values represented by the system and the staff. School work and educational pursuits, for instance, are viewed as fruitless or a waste of
time. They are usually resentful and hostile, and their attitude sets
the tone of the institution for other residents.

---

*Each cottage in both institutions has four wings. It is customary
for each wing to be led by a "bruiser." While power struggles take
place in the microstructure, the four "bruisers" seem to cooperate
with each other in running the cottage.

All youths must take the presence and opinion of bruisers into consideration before they act, since there is no escape from their aggressive and predatory nature. In this society of captives, the bruiser is clearly the king; this youth is the enemy of the staff and the hero of fellow peers. And most of the problems in the cottage arise from their defiant leadership.

DISCUSSION

In the two juvenile correctional institutions examined here, the data support the contention that inmates display different modes of adaptation to incarceration. Utilizing the juvenile's age, sex, race, body size and stature, and dominance in the inmate pecking order, it is possible to match certain juvenile types and adjustment schemes. It is obvious that the dominant, rebellious juvenile, commonly called the bruiser, exercises much authority in the inmate society. Most peers fear these youths far more than any staff member.

The innovators are the master manipulators in the institution. Even though they are relatively unsuccessful in conning staff, they succeed much more often in conning peers. In fact, much of their time is spent exploiting peers. They submerge themselves in the exploitation matrix, constantly attempting to enrich themselves in a politics of scarcity.

The ritualists are the most immature and superficial of the game players. These youths constantly seek the attention of others, show excessive emotion, and even exaggerate their delinquent records. They go through the motions of conning both students and staff, but they are more successful with staff than peers. Fellow residents obviously know "where these youth are coming from" and are not amenable to their tactics. Staff members, especially inexperienced ones, are more receptive to the conning skills of these institutionalized youths.

The retreatists represent a sad situation. These inmates certainly do not belong in the milieu of juvenile correctional institutions. Part of their problem is their seeming inability to defend themselves in this environment—thus resulting in their victimization. Indeed, these youths are likely to become the scapegoats of the entire cottage and frequently are sexually exploited by peers. (Both staff and residents claim that sexual exploitation has decreased since the two institutions have become coeducational. Homosexuality, especially, was rampant at the training school B until boys were transferred to this setting.) If these victims have the chance, they will abscond or otherwise try to withdraw and avoid their threatening environment.

The conformists do not fit in correctional settings any more than the retreatists, but their fate is quite different. They are able

to demonstrate to staff that they are ready to return to community living. They also do not try to con peers or staff members. These
youths tend to be protected by staff because of their conformity to
staff's values. But, since the protection of staff is quite limited in
an institutional context, it is apparent that conformists are able to
protect themselves more effectively than the victimized retreatists.

      The results of this study appear to have certain social policy
implications. Only a few years ago the concept of community-based
corrections and diversionary programming was the focus of nearly
everyone interested in juvenile corrections. Commitments to juvenile correctional facilities were at an all-time low in the late 1960s
and early 1970s. Many students of juvenile corrections thought that
the millennium was at hand and that the day of the training school was
ended (Conrad, 1975). However, the population of training schools
again began to rise in 1975, and it soon became evident that the "hard
line" approach to misbehaving juveniles was gaining public support.
As the media spotlighted the rise and violence of youth crime, the reaction of a growing number of citizens was to demand less permissive-
ness and more punishment for juvenile lawbreakers.

      The consequences of this "let's get tough with the criminal" men-
tality is that training schools are being used at the present time as
much as they ever have been. Nevertheless, our training schools remain inhumane, brutal, and violent settings for wayward youth. Some
youths are sexually exploited and lose their self-respect in these settings; others decide that suicide is the only way out; and still others
leave full of rage because they feel months or years of their lives have
been wasted. In addition, juvenile correctional institutions—private
as well as state—serve as effective schools of crime because graduates
tend to leave more committed to a delinquent career.

      Part of the problem in reforming training schools is the lack of
a unifying philosophy or social policy on how to "correct" juvenile
offenders. Should our child-saving philosophy be based on referral,
reformation, revenge, restraint, or reintegration? Another serious
problem is that traditionally juvenile institutions have been a "disposal
unit" to wash children of the dispossessed down the drain (Forer, 1967).
We have worked very hard in saving the middle-class offender and in
keeping this youth in the community, but the children of the poor are
relegated to institutions. A third problem is the lack of a humanistic
ethic pervading the juvenile justice system. Lisa Richette noted,
"The system [juvenile justice] as a whole has a clinical coldness
about it" (1969, p. 77). Staff in juvenile institutions all too often communicate an indifferent or callous attitude toward their charges.

      This study of training schools in a southern state illustrates
many of the above problems of institutionalizing juveniles. Residents
in this state are more concerned about playing games with staff and

peers than they are with their own growth and development; in fact, they see this game behavior as a necessary means of survival. Some incarcerated youth do not do very well in adapting and end up as scapegoats—ostracized by both peers and staff. The most antisocial youths, the rebels, control the cottage environment by driving home the point effectively that only the strong survive. Finally, the closed society that inmates create is much worse than the one from which they have come. The contention that treatment or rehabilitation can take place in this milieu borders on the absurd.

Two characteristics of this statewide system of training schools merit elaboration. The first is that status offenders continue to be placed in institutions in this state. The researchers were startled, appalled, and dismayed after their contacts with residents in training school B. These adjudicated delinquents actually were small children, some of whom were ten years old. The vast majority of these unfortunate youngsters have been "sent away" for very minor status offenses. In comparing what they have done and the punishment meted out to them, it is clear that no social justice exists for these youths. This institution teaches the lesson well that we must keep status offenders out of the juvenile justice system.

The coeducational nature of all seven training schools in this state, including two diagnostic centers, deserves some praise. The impact of coeducational facilities can be seen from both training schools. Before training school A became coeducational, girls occupying this facility flaunted their sexual relations with each other. Interviewees confirmed that a large number were involved in homosexual relationships. After the arrival of boys at the institution, almost all the girls switched their attention to the newcomers. The same thing happened at training school B when girls were transferred to this middle-of-the-line male institution. Although frequent rapes and sexual assaults had characterized the life of this male institution, the presence of girls changed this behavior; male inmates now claim that very little homosexual behavior is taking place in the cottage. In addition to reducing homosexuality, coeducational institutions seem to add a noticeably warmer and more normal affect to the atmosphere of both training schools.

The basic mission of juvenile corrections is to keep youth in trouble from returning to the juvenile justice system. Needless to say, we have a long way to go to accomplish this mission. Indeed, once youthful offenders are processed through the correctional funnel the chances of their returning are raised instead of reduced. The sad truth is that juvenile corrections appears to breed rather than reform offenders. To minimize the damage of training schools to their occupants, let us try to make them as humane, normal, and homelike as possible. And, by all means, we must keep all but the most delinquent and committed to juvenile crime out of our training schools.

REFERENCES

Barker, Gordon H., and W. Thomas Adams. 1959. "The Social
    Structure of a Correctional Institution." Journal of Criminal
    Law, Criminology and Police Science 49 (January–February):
    416–22.

Bartollas, Clemens, Stuart J. Miller, and Simon Dinitz. 1975.
    "Staff Exploitation of Inmates: The Paradox of Institutional Con-
    trol." In Exploiters and Exploited: The Dynamics of Victimiza-
    tion, edited by Israel Drapkin and Emilio Viano, pp. 157–68.
    Lexington, Mass.: Lexington Books.

_____. 1976a. "The Exploitation Matrix in a Juvenile Institution."
    International Journal of Criminology and Penology 1 (August 4):
    257–70.

_____. 1976b. Juvenile Victimization: The Institutional Paradox.
    New York: Halsted Press; a Sage publication.

Berne, Eric. 1964. Games People Play. New York: Grove Press.

_____. 1972. What Do You Say After You Say Hello? New York:
    Grove Press.

Clemmer, Donald. 1958. The Prison Community. New York:
    Holt, Rinehart and Winston.

Cole, Stephen, and Harriet Zuckerman. 1964. "Inventory of Empiri-
    cal and Theoretical Studies of Anomie." In Anomie and Deviant
    Behavior, edited by Marshall B. Clinard, pp. 243–313. New
    York: Free Press.

Conrad, John P. 1975. "We Should Never Have Promised a Hospi-
    tal." Federal Probation 39 (December): 3–9.

Davis, Alan. 1968. "Sexual Assaults in the Philadelphia Prison Sys-
    tem and Sheriff's Vans." Trans-action 6 (December): 9–17.

Edwards, Anne R. 1970. "Inmate Adaptations and Socialization in
    the Prison." Sociology 4 (May): 213–25.

Ernst, Franklin H., and William C. Keating, Jr. 1964. "Psychiatric
    Treatment of the California Felon." American Journal of Psy-
    chiatry 120 (April): 974–79.

Fisher, Sethard. 1961. "Social Organization in a Correctional Residence." Pacific Sociological Review 4 (Fall): 87–93.

Forer, Lois. 1967. No One Will Listen: How Our Legal System
   Brutalizes the Youthful Poor. New York: John Day.

Giallombardo, Rose. 1966. Society of Women. New York: Wiley.

Goffman, Erving. 1961. Asylums. Garden City, N.Y.: Doubleday
   Anchor Books.

Heffernan, Esther. 1972. Making It in Prison: The Square, the
   Cool, and the Life. New York: Wiley Interscience.

Huffman, Arthur V. 1961. "Problems Precipitated by Homosexual
   Approaches on Youthful First Offenders." Journal of Social
   Therapy 3–4 (Spring): 170–81.

Irwin, John. 1970. The Felon. Englewood Cliffs, N.J.: Prentice-
   Hall.

Irwin, John, and Donald Cressey. 1962. "Thieves, Convicts, and the
   Inmate Culture." Social Problems 10 (Fall): 142–55.

Kadushin, Alfred. 1968. "Games People Play in Supervision." Social Work 13 (July): 23–32.

McCleery, Richard. 1961a. "Authoritarianism and the Belief System of Incorrigibles." In The Prison: Studies in Institutional
   Organization and Change, edited by Donald Cressey, pp. 260–
   306. New York: Holt, Rinehart and Winston.

_____. 1961b. "Policy Change in Prison Management." In Complex
   Organization: A Sociological Reader, edited by Amitai Etzioni,
   pp. 376–400. New York: Free Press.

McCorkle, Lloyd W. 1962. "Guard-Inmate Relationships in Prison."
   In The Sociology of Punishment and Correction, edited by Norman Johnston, Leonard Savitz, and Marvin Wolfgang, pp. 108–
   15. New York: Wiley.

McCorkle, Lloyd W., and Richard Korn. 1962. "Resocialization
   Within Walls." In The Sociology of Punishment and Correction,
   edited by Norman Johnston, Leonard Savitz, and Marvin Wolfgang, pp. 99–107. New York: Wiley.

Merton, Robert K. 1938. "Social Structure and Anomie." American Sociological Review 1 (October): 672–82.

Miller, Stuart J., Clemens Bartollas, Donald Jennifer, Edward Redd, and Simon Dinitz. 1975. "Games Inmates Play: Notes on Staff Victimization." In Exploiters and Exploited: The Dynamics of Victimization, edited by Israel Drapkin and Emilio Viano, pp. 143–55. Lexington, Mass.: Lexington Books.

Morris, Terrence, Pauline Morris, and Barbara Biely. 1961. "It's the Prisoners Who Run This Prison." Prison Service Journal 11 (January): 3–11.

Polsky, Howard. 1962. Cottage Six—The Social System of Delinquent Boys in Residential Treatment. New York: Russell Sage Foundation.

Richette, Lisa A. 1969. The Throwaway Children. New York: Lippincott.

Schrag, Clarence. 1954. "Leadership Among Prison Inmates." American Sociological Review 19 (February): 37–42.

Street, David, Robert Vinter, and Charles Perrow. 1966. Organization for Treatment. New York: Free Press.

Sykes, Gresham M. 1958. The Society of Captives. Princeton, N.J.: Princeton University Press.

Sykes, Gresham M., and Sheldon L. Messinger. 1960. "The Inmate Social System." In Theoretical Studies in Social Organization in the Prison, edited by Richard Cloward et al., pp. 5–19. New York: Social Science Research Council.

Walker, Warren. 1974. "Games Families of Delinquents Play." In Corrections in the Community, edited by George Killinger and Paul Cromwell, pp. 247–56. St. Paul, Minn.: West.

Ward, David, and Gene Kassebaum. 1965. Women's Prison. Chicago: Aldin.

Wellford, Charles. 1967. "Factors Associated with Adopting the Inmate Code." The Journal of Criminal Law, Criminology and Police Science 58 (June): 197–203.

6

CAN LABELING BE USEFUL?
Gideon Fishman

If one were to sum up the labeling theory in a nutshell, the most proper statement would have been that criminals are the product of the system and are a result of the way our society reacts to deviance and crime. It is, of course, a bit naive and unfair to leave the statement at that without realizing the elaborate processes and mechanisms that are involved in labeling and in the stages of assuming a delinquent identity (Tannenbaum, 1938; Lemert, 1951, 1967; Becker, 1963).

The main tenet of the "labeling theory" is a sociological platitude, namely, that the predicate of "deviance" does not inhere in any form of human behavior but is attributed to it from definable standpoints.

The corollaries associated with the theory are, however, far from trivial. Of these, two are especially noteworthy.

1. The attribution of the predicate of deviance is not an automatic function resulting from the association of forms of behavior and cultural standards; it materializes in labeling processes. Hence, the structures of these processes must be examined.

This research is based on a larger research project that was sponsored by the Program for the Study of Crime and Delinquency at Ohio State University. Appreciation is extended to Simon Dinitz and Joseph E. Scott for their helpful suggestions throughout the research. Appreciation is also extended to Egon Bitnner for his thoughtful comments during the writing of this chapter.

This study appears in a revised version in the International Journal of Criminology and Penology, February 1976.

   2.   Since the labeling process attaches the label to both the activity and the agent, it enhances the likelihood that the labeled agent
will adopt a deviant "identity" in accordance with the looking-glass
theory of identity formation.

   Thus, the criminal justice system is much at fault in creating
or at least reinforcing its own clients. However, this account, real-
istic as it may be, is conceptually and empirically oversimplified.
If Edwin Lemert's (1951, p. 75; 1967, pp. 46-49) account for the
emergence of delinquency is to be taken literally, most delinquents
who have been processed through the juvenile system of correction—
either detention, court appearance, or institutionalization—should
reach the stage of secondary deviance. The latter is characterized
by the juvenile's realization that there is no use in changing his behavior patterns since others have already determined that he is "no
good." Thus, he may as well continue with his already-defined negative behavior. This is also consistent with the way self-perception
and self-images are established (Goffman, 1963, pp. 91-98). A secondary deviance stage occurs, then, only after official contact with
a legal agency has taken place, after which a delinquent role is supposed to be assumed on a full-time basis.
   The questions under study here are as follows:

   1.   Do all, or even most, boys after an official contact with a
legal law enforcement agency really adopt a negative self-perception?
   2.   Does a negative self-perception necessarily lead to further
delinquent and law-breaking behavior?

                        RESEARCH DESIGN

   This research was conducted at a juvenile delinquency treatment center in a Midwestern state. It is an open setup for delinquents
and mildly disturbed youth with the population reaching 25 boys at
any given time.* All boys who resided at the institution, from its in-
ception in 1961 until the beginning of 1973, were included as potential
subjects. The total number of boys was 137. Out of this total population two refused to cooperate in the research, and 34 neither responded
nor were accessible to personal contact. Three of the potential subjects are deceased, and 38 other potential subjects were never actually contacted because of incorrect mailing addresses. Thus we
were left with 63 respondents.

─────────────────────────
   *Recently the institution has been extended and is able to house
up to 50 boys.

A questionnaire schedule was designed and handed to the subjects when personal contact could be established. It was mailed to those subjects with whom it was impossible—due to distance—to make personal contact. The schedule included questions as to the subject's deviant self-perception, the way he thought others perceived him, and whether he felt he had been denied a job because of his past record. These questions constituted a labeling scale with a reliability of 0.80 on the Kuder-Richardson scale (Formula 8).

Other indexes and scales were also utilized to obtain postrelease information, which served as an overall adjustment sensor. The subject's criminal involvement was determined by an index based on a self-reported schedule consisting of 30 criminal and deviant activities.* The offenses were ranked—serious, moderate, minor—by their degree of seriousness as derived from their legal definitions. An arbitrary weighting system was used so the number of serious violations per subject was multiplied by a factor of three, moderate offenses by a factor of two, and minor events by a factor of one. The researcher was able to obtain from police files the absolute number of prison recommitments and was able to calculate the length of reinstitutionalization per subject.

Another variable that was of major interest was job adjustment. A scale that contained four dichotomized (yes, no) items—employment (full- or part-time); job satisfaction; promotions; plans to stay on the job—was devised; it produced a very high reliability coefficience, +.85 on the Kuder-Richardson scale (Formula 8).

The last variable that was investigated refers to one's level of what we called self-development. The self-development index consisted of a set of seven questions dealing with one's ability to deal better with everyday problems, keep one's "cool" in uneasy situations, come to a better understanding with one's family, spend time in a useful manner, keep out of trouble with the police, get a job, and be responsible for one's own behavior.

Each of these items was scaled from one to three, with one meaning yes, two meaning don't know, and three meaning no. The responses were summed for each individual. These totals were displayed in a frequency distribution of scores ranging from 7 to 21. Obviously, the lower the score the more successful the self-development process seems to have been.

It was the purpose of this research to find out whether the traditional labeling hypothesis is factual; namely, that once one comes in

———————————

*The self-reported schedule is similar to the one used by M. Wolfgang in his Cohort Analysis and by the Presidential Commission for the Study of Juvenile Delinquency.

touch, let alone processed through the justice system, the juvenile assumes a delinquent identity and proceeds into a delinquent way of life. The theoretical question at stake is as follows: If the hypothesis is true, one would expect to find among the delinquents a negative self-perception. This, in turn, is supposed to have a devastating influence on further adjustment in the community.

FINDINGS AND ANALYSIS

Examining each of the various indexes separately, one learns that over two-thirds of the respondents were employed, while only a little over a quarter of all respondents were unemployed. Moreover, the overall job adjustment was much lower. Only 69 (46.0 percent) were well adjusted in their jobs (Table 6.1). Only 17 (27.0 percent) had reached a high level of self-development, while the mode reveals low level of self-development.

As to recommitments, almost 70 percent were not recommitted; and, of the remaining 30 percent who were recommitted, 7 (11.1 percent) were recommitted for a period of up to one year, and 12 (19.1 percent) were recommitted for a period of over one year. The over one year commitment indicates serious criminal involvement. In addition, those who were aware of the labeling effect are clearly distinguishable from those who were unaware.

Finally, Table 6.1 reveals that 32 subjects, less than one-third, had reported low criminal involvement. This, however, is a rather vague and general description that can be better clarified by the information offered in Table 6.2.

Looking at the total number of offenses, it becomes evident that only three exinstitutionalized subjects had not committed any offense. This is a striking figure by any standard, keeping in mind, though, that it refers to all types of offenses—serious and minor. When these three different levels of offenses were examined, it became apparent that the minor offenses made very little difference and increased the total number of self-reported participants in crime only by one additional case. This is deduced through the fact that only four subjects had not been involved in moderate types of offenses, as opposed to three in the minor offense category. On the other hand, 25 (39.7 percent) had not reported the commission of any major crime since their release.

The next step in our analysis was to find if there were any relationships between the above-described indexes of adjustment and the labeling phenomenon. The measurements of association were chi-square tests of significance and Pearson correlation coefficients, as presented in Table 6.3.

TABLE 6.1

Indexes of Adjustment of 63 Exdelinquent Boys

Index of Adjustment	Respondents	
	N	Percent
Job adjustment		
Good	29	46.0
Poor	20	31.8
W/A	14	22.2
Self-development		
High	17	21.0
Moderate	21	33.3
Low	25	39.7
Number of recommitments		
None	44	69.8
One or more	19	30.2
Length of recommitment		
No recommitment	44	69.8
Up to a year	7	11.1
Over a year	12	19.1
Labeling effect		
Definite effect	21	33.3
Undeterminate effect	19	30.2
No effect	23	36.5
Criminal involvement after release		
(self-reported)		
Low	32	50.8
High	31	49.2

Source: Compiled by the author.

The statistical nonsignificance of most chi-square values and correlation coefficients is important and reflects on the validity of the traditional hypothesis, which suggests that the labeling process is universal following trouble with the law and that it has a detrimental effect on the ability of one to adjust in the community. As a minimum, confirming data for such a hypothesis should show a high rate of recidivism and, additionally, show significant negative relationships between all adjustment indexes and the labeling effect. This was clearly not the case. The only significant findings are to be found in the relations between length of recommitment and labeling effect, which contradict the expected relationships.

TABLE 6.2

Type of Postinstitutional Offenses by Number of Offenses

Number of Offenses	Minor		Moderate		Serious		All Combined	
	Number	Percent	Number	Percent	Number	Percent	Number	Percent
0	3	4.8	4	6.3	25	39.7	3	4.8
1+	60	95.2	59	93.7	38	63.3	60	95.2
Total	63	100.0	63	100.0	63	100.0	63	100.0

Source: Compiled by the author.

Although the variable, length of recommitment, is only one indicator of several indexes and indicators that deal with overall community adjustment, it appears that the length of recommitment is indicative also of the seriousness of the offenses one commits. In this respect its high correlation with the labeling effect is highly meaningful and theoretically important. Statistically, the correlation shows that the length of recommitment and, thus, the seriousness of the offense, is positively correlated with unawareness of labeling effect. The less labeling effect there is, the longer the reinstitutionalization and, by the same token, the more serious the crime.

TABLE 6.3

Relationships Between Labeling Effect and Adjustment Indexes

Index of Adjustment	Labeling Effect	
	x^2	Pearson Correlation
Job adjustment	n.s.	−.09
Self-development	n.s.	−.18
Criminal involvement after release	n.s.	−.007
Number of recommitments	n.s.	−.04
Length of recommitment	11.21	+.72

Note: n.s. = not significant.

Source: Compiled by the author.

DISCUSSION

From our findings, with all due reservation as to our small sample and its limited generalizability, it is evident that the labeling hypothesis must be reappraised and reexamined for its limits to be determined. It must be questioned, first, whether the secondary deviance stage is actually as universal as some claim. Second, is it as automatic and mechanistic as described in the literature (Cicourel, 1968; Lemert, 1951, 1967; Tannenbaum, 1938; Becker, 1963)? In other words, the question that is raised by our findings is: Do all boys who are processed through the juvenile justice system develop a negative, or a delinquent, self-identity? The data presented here clearly show that this is not the case. The second question, realizing that some boys actually did perceive themselves as delinquents, is whether the offense rate of those was higher than that of juveniles who did not have a delinquent identity. The findings dispute this as well. The overall adjustment rate in the community, including future involvement in crime, was not associated with the labeling effect. The single variable that was significantly related with the labeling effect was the length of recommitment (which also indicates the seriousness of the offense committed after release from the institution). However, the relationship here contradicted expectations. The more serious offenders, those who were recommitted for longer terms, were not those who seem to have experienced the labeling effect but rather those who were not affected by the labeling process, at least according to the youths' own perceptions.

The possible explanation of these findings would suggest four hypotheses. First, the labeling effect is differentially felt, and sometimes is not felt at all, by juveniles who have been processed through the juvenile justice system. Second, those who do experience the negative labeling effect are not always adopting a criminal mode of behavior. Third, awareness of the labeling effect may indicate sensitivity to informal social controls and awareness of the "significant other" (Mead, 1934, p. 155; Cooley, 1964, p. 182), who is a member of the law-abiding population. Fourth, lack of awareness as to the existence of the labeling effect may suggest a lack in sensitivity to informal social controls and the irrelevance of the law-abiding reference group.

These hypotheses would lead us to offer a revision of the traditional labeling hypothesis. Thus, it should be pointed out that juveniles who have been formally processed through the court system, who fail to recognize that labeling has occurred and thus exhibit closure to the influence of law-abiding reference groups and their informal control power, will engage in continuous criminal behavior. On the other hand, juveniles who have been processed through the court

system, who perceive the fact of being negatively labeled and hurt,
and who thus indicate acceptance of community controls, will try to
stay away from adopting a criminal way of life.

These two types of reaction to labeling probably represent the
majority of the cases. However, it is evident that some of the subjects who did perceive themselves as subjected to the labeling effect
did, in fact, continue their negative and law-breaking behavior. This
pattern is the only one that conforms to the common labeling hypothesis. It, as indicated by our data, represents only the minority of
cases and probably refers to those youngsters who are at a stage of
desperation as to their chances for rehabilitation and make a conscious
decision to adopt a deviant way of life.

The implications of these findings could reach beyond the refinement that it offers to the traditional labeling perspective. It points
out that labeling is not to be universally perceived as having a negative and devastating effect on the juvenile. For certain boys, labeling
can, indeed, serve as a control mechanism that regulates their behavior. For them, the stigma that results from the labeling process
is a signal as to the tolerance limits of the community.

These findings should be used in policy implementation concerning "good risks" to be released from confinement. One should be
more careful with the insensitives who do not realize the community
dissatisfaction and the negative reaction to criminal behavior. By
the same token, the more sensitive youth who is deterred from further
delinquency after realizing the negative reaction such behavior promotes in the community must be identified. The identification of
those who are potential recidivists and who do not make an attempt to
refrain from criminal behavior must be made. All these assessments
must be made if the "hard core" delinquents are not to enter the "good
risk" group. It is in the refinement of these distinctions that practical
use of the inevitable labeling can be most productive.

REFERENCES

Becker, Howard S. 1963. Outsiders: Studies in the Sociology of De-
        viance. Glencoe, Ill.: Free Press of Glencoe.

Cicourel, Aaron V. 1968. The Social Organization of Juvenile Jus-
        tice. New York: Wiley.

Cooley, Charles H. 1964. Human Nature and the Social Order. New
        York: Shocken.

Goffman, Erving. 1963. Stigma. Englewood Cliffs, N.J.: Prentice-
        Hall.

Lemert, Edwin M. 1951. Social Pathology. New York: McGraw–Hill.

_____. 1967. Human Deviance, Social Problems and Social Control. Englewood Cliffs, N.J.: Prentice-Hall.

Mead, George H. 1934. Mind, Self and Society. Chicago: University of Chicago Press.

Tannenbaum, Frank. 1938. Crime and the Community. New York: Columbia University Press.

7

WHO WILL RETURN?
SOCIAL AND LEGAL
CORRELATES OF
JUVENILE RECIDIVISM
Charles W. Thomas

INTRODUCTION

The assertions of some labeling theorists notwithstanding, the majority of individuals who appear before our juvenile and adult courts do not reappear. Predicting who will and who will not reappear, however, has proven to be an exceedingly difficult task. Yet recidivism remains such a sufficiently important issue that a continuation of research on the topic is clearly warranted. Such research, for example, can do much to stimulate the development of more sophisticated models that are capable of accounting for persistent as well as transitory involvement in criminality and delinquency. Further, the contradictory predictions of labeling theory advocates who view the imposition of formal legal sanctions as a contingency that promotes a movement toward secondary deviance* and proponents of social con-

---

*Edwin Lemert, Thomas Scheff, and a variety of other contemporary advocates of the labeling perspective have suggested that the

===

The author wishes to express his appreciation for the assistance provided by Robin J. Cage of the College of William and Mary during the preparation of this chapter and to Betty Wade Coyle and Ronald Collier, also of the College of William and Mary, for their assistance in the collection of the data presented in the analysis. This research was supported by grant 75-NI-99-0031 from the Law Enforcement Assistance Administration. This financial support, however, does not necessarily indicate the concurrence of LEAA in any of the statements or conclusions contained in the chapter.

trol or deterrence conceptualizations who argue that formal sanctions have a specific deterrent effect* can be directly addressed within the context of research on recidivism.

Further still, the relevance of recidivism research to those with applied interests is obvious. Members of the judiciary, for example, have a direct interest in such research on at least two levels. They are immediately concerned with the likelihood that an individual who appears before them will subsequently reappear. Second, they have at least an equal concern with the relative efficacy of the various dispositional alternatives that are at their disposal. Similarly, correctional practitioners whose responsibilities lie in the areas of probation, parole, or institutional care have a considerable interest in both predicting the outcome of their intervention and defining high and low risk categories of the offender population prior to determining the type of intervention, if any, which is appropriate.

In view of the theoretical and practical relevance of recidivism, the relative paucity of sound empirical research and predictive models stands as something of a paradox. Although the shortage of previous work is a limiting factor, the purpose of this chapter, which is one of a series coming from a larger project that is focusing on the im-

---

imposition of sanctions, particularly formal legal sanctions, encourage the development of career deviance. The point is made most explicitly, however, by the following quote from the discussion provided by Frank Tannenbaum in his now-classic Crime and the Community (1938) that is cited in a recent examination of labeling theory by R. Hawkins and G. Tiedeman (1975, p. 44):

> The process of making the criminal, therefore, is a process of tagging, defining, identifying, segregating, describing, emphasizing, making conscious and self-conscious; it becomes a way of stimulating, suggesting, emphasizing, and evoking the very traits complained of. . . .
> The person becomes the thing he is described as being.
> [Emphasis added.]

*Regardless of whether the origins of contemporary deterrence models are linked to the works of the classical school of criminology, reinforcement learning theory, the rationalistic assumptions of many economic models, or sociological examinations of social control, such models are in many ways a direct contradiction of the most basic assertions of the labeling approach. For a lengthy and current bibliography of theoretical and empirical research on deterrence, see Thomas and Williams (1974)

pact of legal processing and formal legal sanctions on juvenile delinquency, * is to evaluate the ability of juvenile court officials to predict
recidivism on the basis of information they routinely attempt to obtain on juveniles at the point of their first appearance in juvenile
court. [†]

PREVIOUS RESEARCH

The preponderance of previously reported research on recidivism
among juveniles has focused on official reactions to those who had
been released from some type of institutional care (Mannheim and Wilkins, 1955; Arbuckle and Litwack, 1960; Laulicht, 1962, 1963; Scott,
1964; Little, 1965; Cockett, 1967; Baer, 1970; Uusitalo, 1972; Miller
and Dinitz, 1973; Rosenberg, 1973; Buikhuisen and Hoekstra, 1974;
Eysenck and Eysenck, 1974; Sepsi, 1974). Not unlike the more immediately relevant research on less restrictively defined populations,
varying definitions of recidivism make any comparison of the findings
contained in this body of literature problematic. D. S. Arbuckle and
L. Litwack (1960, p. 45), for example, define the term quite restrictively as a "(p)erson on parole from a training institution who is returned to the institution for violation of parole, who is recommitted
by the courts, or who appears in a higher court while on parole and
subsequently is sentenced to another institution." Others develop
definitions based on reconviction (Scott, 1964; Cockett, 1967; Buikhuisen and Hoekstra, 1974; Eysenck and Eysenck, 1974), frequently
including a specific time interval within which reconviction must occur. Scott (1964, p. 527), for example, defines a recidivist as a juvenile whose record shows "(a) further finding of guilt within three
years of release." However useful this body of literature might be to

---

*Of the several recent research reports that have been prepared
as part of this larger study, the most immediately relevant are those
by Thomas and Cage (1975) and Thomas, Kreps, and Cage (1975).

[†]It should be carefully noted that some types of information are
most frequently obtained when the juvenile has a prior offense record
or when the alleged offense is serious. For example, the two jurisdictions within which the data for this study were collected often
failed to gather information on such variables as school attendance,
social adjustment in school, home situation, and socioeconomic status
when the first offense was not particularly serious. Thus, the mere
presence of these types of data in the official records suggests that
the case was defined as relatively serious.

those who wish to evaluate the impact of confinement or specific
types of treatment modalities on juveniles who have been committed
for institutional supervision, it provides little relevant information
for those concerned with recidivism among youths who appear before
juvenile courts.

This is not to suggest that no attention has been focused on recidivism at the level of juvenile court operations. Particularly in recent years there appears to have been an increasing level of interest
in this topic, an interest that is attested to by reports from the United
States (Hutcheson et al., 1966; Unkovic and Ducsay, 1969; Thornberry,
1971; Ferster and Courtless, 1972; Meade, 1973), England (Knight and
West, 1975), and Australia (Kraus, 1970, 1973a, 1973b; Kraus and
Smith, 1973). Thus, a brief review of selected studies is instructive.

C. M. Unkovic and W. J. Ducsay (1969) report the findings of a
predictive attribute analysis that they conducted using a series of 12
variables abstracted from the official court records of 2,548 juveniles
who appeared before the Cleveland, Ohio, juvenile courts between 1956
and 1965. Six of these variables were significantly linked to recidivism:
younger offenders, males, those whose offense involved a victim,
blacks, Protestants, and those who committed an offense in the presence of other juveniles were most likely to become recidivists. The
typological method they employed identified 18 groups of juveniles
with percentages of recidivism that ranged from a low of 16 percent
to a high of 73 percent.

Unfortunately, methodological shortcomings in the analysis reported in this study diminishes its utility. Like the preponderance
of research on recidivism, including the present report, Unkovic and
Ducsay (1969) were forced to rely on official records as their data
source. The inherent problems presented by such records are well-
known and require no detailed comment here. In addition, however,
no operational definition of recidivism beyond an indication that they
examined "records on recidivism over a ten-year period from Juvenile Court hearings" (1969, p. 340) is provided. Whether this refers
to multiple court appearances, multiple adjudications, or a combination of appearances and adjudications cannot be determined. Even
more important, no control is reported to adjust for variations in the
amount of risk time to which each juvenile was exposed. The significance of this flaw is considerable. An eight-year-old juvenile offender who came before the court in 1956 (and who continued to reside
in the Cleveland area) was exposed to a full ten years of risk, but if
the same child were to have appeared in 1965 he would have only confronted a maximum risk period of one year. Further, on the average, older offenders were exposed to relatively less risk than younger
offenders. A 17-year-old, for example, whose first appearance fell
in any of the years sampled could be a risk for no more than one year

(after which he would be treated as an adult and not included in the data source employed). Thus, the finding that younger offenders were more likely to recidivate might reflect either a tendency for those whose initial appearance in court comes at a relatively young age or the fact that the younger elements in the sample were at risk for a longer period of time than was true for their counterparts, who were relatively older at the time of their first appearance.

Many of the methodological problems that undermine the Unkovic and Ducsay research were dealt with more effectively in a recent study conducted by A. Meade (1973) on 439 juveniles who had been randomly selected from a universe of 8,476 cases on whom official records were available in "a large southeastern metropolitan area" (1973, p. 478) during 1968-70. Data were obtained on the age, sex, race, social class, family structure, type of first offense, disposition of first offense, and recidivism status of each case. The subsequent behavior of each juvenile was monitored for a period of at least 18 months after initial appearance.* Recidivism was defined as a delin-quent offense that resulted in the filing of an official petition. Meade found that status offenders, juveniles who were relatively older at the time of their initial court appearance, those who were school failures, and those who were subjected to a formal court appearance at the time of their first offense (that came to the attention of juvenile court officials) were more likely to recidivate (67 percent of those who had all four of these traits were recidivists as opposed to only 8 percent of those who had none of these traits). Race, sex, social class (as measured by the economic status of the census block in which the juvenile resided), and whether the juvenile's home was dis-rupted were not significantly linked to recidivism.

Finally, a series of studies conducted by J. Kraus (1970, 1973a, 1973b) and Kraus and J. Smith (1973) provide additional information on juvenile recidivism, even though potential variations in judicial policies, statutory provisions, and offender populations must be taken into consideration in assessing the relevance of research conducted outside the United States. In 1970, for example, Kraus reported the findings of a project that focused on recidivism among a sample of

---

*This monitoring procedure significantly reduces the risk of time bias noted in the work of Unkovic and Ducsay by specifying a minimum risk period, but the minimum period appears rather short. Moreover, no controls were reported to adjust for the fact that some elements in the sample were presumably at risk for a period in excess of 18 months. Still, because Meade employed the same basic definition of recidivism as is used in this study, his research provides a direct point of com-parison between earlier research and the present analysis.

juveniles placed on probation by New South Wales juvenile courts during 1962 and 1963. Data were obtained over a five-year period on the offense records of seven separate offense groupings, each of which included 50 juveniles subsequent to their placement on probation. Some of those in the sample had prior offense records at the beginning of the study; some did not. Three separate indicators of recidivism were employed: the occurrence of a new offense, the rate of offenses committed during the follow-up period, and imprisonment for a new offense after being assigned to probation supervision. The primary object of the analysis presented was the determination of the impact of probation supervision on recidivism. Kraus's findings reveal no association between duration of supervision and recidivism nor between age at first offense, age at time of placement on probation, or rural versus urban residence and recidivism. A significant link was found between prior criminal record and recidivism. Further, when recidivism rates between the seven offense groupings were compared, the differences were significant (a group comparable to status offenders had the highest probability of recidivating; sex offenders were least likely to recidivate). Later, Kraus and Smith (1973) examined the effect of family structure on recidivism among a sample of 1,130 males who appeared before the Sidney Children's Court during 1970. That analysis revealed recidivism to be most likely to occur in "father only" homes and that "mother only" were more likely to contain recidivists than homes in which two parents were present.

These and other relevant studies provide us with inconsistent leads as to how recidivism can best be predicted. Thornberry (1971), for example, found that race and socioeconomic status were predictors of recidivism; Unkovic and Ducsay (1969) suggest that race is a predictor, but that socioeconomic status is not; Meade (1973) found that neither race nor socioeconomic status predicts recidivism. Similarly, sex of the offender was a viable predictor for Unkovic and Ducsay, but not for Meade; B. J. Knight and D. J. West (1975) found no relationship between personality measures and recidivism, but B. R. Hutcheson et al. (1966) found that subjective psychiatric judgments were the only sound predictors; Knight and West found more serious subsequent offenses among those who reported having committed a delinquent act by themselves, but Unkovic and Ducsay found that the opposite held among those in their sample. And so it goes. Virtually no variables, with the possible exception of offense type and prior offense record, show a consistent association with recidivism.

In the face of both this inconsistency and the absence of even the most rudimentary theoretical models, researchers are necessarily left in a position that requires them to reduce as many of the methodological problems as they can while conducting analysis that can only be described as highly atheoretical and exploratory. That is exactly

the approach taken in this study. The research hypotheses are necessarily tentative because of the contradictory leads that can be derived
from the previously reported literature, but there appears to be direct or indirect support for the following expectations:

　　1. Regarding the social and demographic characteristics of juvenile offenders, those who are younger at the time of their first court
appearance, males, and blacks will be more likely to recidivate than
their counterparts;
　　2. Regarding the social circumstances of juvenile offenders,
those from lower socioeconomic strata and disrupted homes will be
more likely to recidivate than those who lack these characteristics;
　　3. Regarding the social adjustment and behavioral characteristics of juvenile offenders, those who are not in school, who present
behavioral problems if they are in school, and who have not actively
been involved in religious activities will be more likely to recidivate
than others in the offender population; and
　　4. Regarding legal and quasi-legal variables, those who committed a solitary rather than a group-related delinquent act, who committed a status offense, and who received a relatively harsh disposition at the time of their initial court appearance will be more likely to
recidivate than others in the sample.

Numerous other hypotheses could be advanced, of course, but only
those expectations that could be evaluated with the data presently
available are presented.

RESEARCH METHODOLOGY

　　The data employed in the analysis that follows were obtained
from a subsample of cases that had been abstracted from the official
court records of two urban juvenile court jurisdictions that are located within a single Standard Metropolitan Stastical Area in the
southeast: Portsmouth and Virginia Beach, Virginia. The original
sample consists of randomly selected records on juveniles who appeared before these courts between January 1, 1970, and December
31, 1974. Every fourth case to appear before the Virginia Beach
court on the basis of a petition alleging delinquent behavior was selected; every third case was chosen in Portsmouth because of the relatively lower number of cases processed in that jurisdiction during the
time period under examination. This set of data, however, included
information on juveniles who: (1) were not residents of the jurisdiction in which their case(s) appeared; (2) had first appearances prior
to 1970; (3) appeared at an initial and/or adjudicatory hearing, but

not a dispositional hearing; and (4) received a disposition, primarily commitment to institutional supervision, that made a precise measurement of the time period during which they could have recidivated impossible. Thus, it was necessary to restrict this analysis of recidivism to the data obtained on 1,702 juveniles who were residents of the area, whose first appearance in court took place during the sampling period, whose cases were officially disposed of, and for whom exact risk time could be quantified. The manner in which the major variables were operationalized is described below.

Although all data were coded in the manner that they appeared on the court records, a good deal of categorization of the raw data had to be accomplished to perform the analysis. To provide a means by which the correlations reported in the analysis can be interpreted, it is necessary to specify the manner in which recoding was conducted. For the dichotomous variables of sex, race, disrupted homes, school attendance, school behavior, and group versus solitary delinquency, the arbitrary weights assigned were as follows: females, blacks, those from homes in which both parents were present, those who were still attending school, those whose behavior in school was described as average to good, and those who had no codefendants (solitary delinquent acts) were assigned values of "1"; their counterparts a value of "2." The type of offense at first court appearance variable was trichotomized into felonies, status offenses, and misdemeanors on the basis of existing Virginia statutes. Values of "1," "2," and "3" were assigned to these categories. Level of religious activity was also trichotomized: 1 = very active; 2 = moderately active; and 3 = not active. Dispositions of first offenses were classified into four categories: 1 = case dismissed or nolle processed; 2 = case continued generally; 3 = fine or restitution required; 4 = some type of supervision required other than institutionalization, primarily standard supervised probation. Socioeconomic status was divided into five ordered categories on the basis of the occupational rating scale developed by Hollingshead (1958), with the fifth category including the lower three classifications described by Hollingshead. The lower the value of this measure, the higher the socioeconomic status. Six categories were created for age at first court appearance. The lowest value was assigned to those who were 12 years old or less at first appearance, and separate ordered categories were used for those who were 13 to 17 years old. Recidivism was dichotomized; a value of "1" was assigned to those who had no subsequent court appearances; a "2" to those with one or more subsequent appearances. Finally, to control for variations in the length of time during which each juvenile could have recidivated, a risk variable was created by determining the number of months between each juvenile's first court appearance and the end of the sampling period and the number of months between age at

first appearance and 18th birthday. For those in the sample whose
18th birthday occurred prior to the end of the sampling period, months
of risk were set equal to the latter computation; for all others the former number of months was employed. This risk-months distribution
was then dichotomized at its median: 18 months. Those with less
than the median number of months at risk were assigned a risk variable value of "1," and all others a value of "2."

ANALYSIS AND FINDINGS

The purpose of the analysis is to address a series of related
issues that are associated with the general problem of recidivism.
The initial and most basic problem is to determine which variables
facilitate the prediction of recidivism. Assuming that these predictor
variables can be identified, it is essential that we introduce a control
for the potentially biasing effect of varying periods during which individual juveniles could have recidivated. Indeed, simple logic as well
as prior research on both juveniles and adults would imply that the
longer an individual's behavior is monitored, the higher the probability
that he will become defined as a recidivist. More important, however,
it is necessary to determine whether generally useful predictors of
recidivism take on more or less important roles when the length of
risk time is held constant. In addition, attention will be focused on
the extent to which significant predictors of recidivism can be usefully
merged into a single variable that is capable of identifying categories
of juveniles who are most and least likely to recidivate. Finally, the
analysis will conclude with an assessment of the relative importance
of each predictor variable.

Before turning attention toward these more complex undertak-
ings, a brief overview of the basic findings of our analysis is appropriate to communicate something about the type and magnitude of the
recidivism problem that confronts the two court jurisdictions within
which data were obtained. Specifically, 28.7 percent of those in our
sample of juveniles whose first court appearance took place between
1970 and 1974 also reappeared at one or more points during that time
period. Thus, almost one out of every three juveniles who appeared
once during the five-year period recidivated during that same period.
As expected, the overall probability of reappearance was strongly
influenced by the duration of the risk period that each juvenile confronted (Yule's Q = .412). The median number of months between
first appearance and either the juvenile's 18th birthday or the end of
the sampling period (the smaller of the two was used as our measure
of time at risk) was 18 months. The probability of recidivism among
those with less than the median number of months at risk was lower

than the overall rate of 28.7 per hundred appearances (19.6 per hundred), but the rate was significantly higher for those with longer than the median period at risk (36.9 per hundred).

In interpreting these relatively high recidivism rates it is essential that the reader recall that our sampling procedures quite probably had the net effect of making our estimates of recidivism conservative. For example, relying on official court records rather than actual behavioral measures produces lower estimates of recidivism than would have been the case otherwise. Further, migration out of the jurisdiction in which the initial court appearance took place largely eliminated the possibility that any subsequent court appearances would be recorded in the data we obtained. Indeed, even among that segment of our sample who were not geographically mobile during the period under examination, subsequent court appearances in another court in the several nearby court jurisdictions would not normally be noted in the records of the initial court. On the other hand, other aspects of our sample design introduced a reverse influence. Juveniles who were not residents of the jurisdiction in which the initial appearance occurred, for example, were excluded from our analysis. In addition, juveniles who were committed for institutional supervision who were residents were also excluded. Finally, our definition of recidivism in terms of multiple court appearances rather than multiple adjudications also tends to increase our estimates of recidivism. On balance, however, both our sample selection procedures and our definition of recidivism appear to represent as meaningful a sociological definition, though not a precise legal definition, of recidivism as could be obtained given the constraints of the data at our disposal.

A more detailed examination of our findings reveals that the probability of recidivism is related to a series of social and legal variables independent of the influence of risk time. Moreover, many of the variables that have statistically significant associations with recidivism are also related to one another. Table 7.1 provides a summary of the magnitude of the overall interrelationships between all variables under study; Table 7.2 focuses on the links between hypothetically meaningful predictor variables and recidivism both before and after the dichotomized time at risk variable is held constant in order to obtain conditional measures of association.

As indicated in both Tables 7.1 and 7.2, the single best predictor is risk time (Yule's Q = .412). The other significant predictors, in order of their magnitude of association, are school behavior (Yule's Q = .374), presence of codefendants at first court appearance (Yule's Q = -.335), age at first court appearance (Yule's Q = -.329), school attendance status (Yule's Q = .232), offense type on first offense (gamma = -.216), type of disposition received at initial appearance

TABLE 7.1

Intercorrelation Matrix

	X1	X2	X3	X4	X5	X6	X7	X8	X9	X10	X11	X12	X13
X1	1.000	.121	-.035	-.528	.003	.054	-.092	-.142	-.727	.176	.359	-.084	-.094
X2	—	1.000	.394	-.157	-.078	.061	-.103	.220	-.106	.066	-.083	.004	.078
X3	—	—	1.000	-.075	-.233	-.128	-.173	.041	.151	-.040	-.128	-.091	-.335
X4	—	—	—	1.000	.154	.116	.062	.094	.279	-.148	.104	-.080	.059
X5	—	—	—	—	1.000	.701	-.131	-.024	.164	-.065	.307	-.115	.374
X6	—	—	—	—	—	1.000	-.024	-.070	.168	.436	.421	-.187	.232
X7	—	—	—	—	—	—	1.000	-.144	.062	.121	-.109	-.102	-.216
X8	—	—	—	—	—	—	—	1.000	-.024	-.115	-.064	.032	.212
X9	—	—	—	—	—	—	—	—	1.000	-.026	-.044	.145	.029
X10	—	—	—	—	—	—	—	—	—	1.000	.099	-.537	-.329
X11	—	—	—	—	—	—	—	—	—	—	1.000	-.004	.210
X12	—	—	—	—	—	—	—	—	—	—	—	1.000	.412
X13	—	—	—	—	—	—	—	—	—	—	—	—	1.000

Note:

X1 = race
X2 = sex
X3 = codefendants
X4 = family situation
X5 = school behavior
X6 = school attendance
X7 = type of first offense

X8 = disposition first offense
X9 = socioeconomic status
X10 = age at first offense
X11 = religious activity
X12 = time at risk
X13 = recidivism

Source: Compiled by the author.

TABLE 7.2

Relationships Between Predictor Variables and Recidivism

| | Variable Categories | | | | | | | | | | | |
| | Social/Demographic | | | Social Context | | Adjustment/Behavior | | | Legal Influences | | | Risk |
	X_1	X_2	X_3	X_4	X_5	X_6	X_7	X_8	X_9	X_{10}	X_{11}	X_{12}
Overall	-.392	-.094*	.078*	.028*	.059*	.232*	.374	.210	-.335	-.216	.212	.412
High risk	-.193	-.167	.132*	.089*	.118*	.287	.393	.149*	-.320	-.174	.149	n.a.
Low risk	-.358	.070*	.003*	-.160*	.021*	.280	.326	.330	-.337	-.249	.312	n.a.

n.a. = not available.

*Indicates relationships not significant at or less than the .05 level.

Note:

X_1 = age
X_2 = race
X_3 = sex
X_4 = socioeconomic status
X_5 = home
X_6 = school attendance

X_7 = school social
X_8 = religious activity
X_9 = codefendants
X_{10} = offense
X_{11} = disposition
X_{12} = risk

Source: Compiled by the author.

(gamma = .212), and level of religious activity (gamma = .210).*
This, in turn, indicates that the rate of recidivism per hundred juveniles was highest among those with above the median number of months
at risk (37.0); those with behavioral problems in school (54.0); those
who had no codefendants at their initial appearance (38.4); those who
were younger at their first court appearance (the highest recidivism
rate was 41.7 per hundred among those who were 13 years old); those
who had dropped out of school (52.2); those charged with a status
offense (42.3); those who were placed on some form of formal supervision by the court after their initial appearance (39.3); and those who
were not active religiously (49.9). [†] Thus, the preponderance of the
exploratory hypotheses advanced earlier are supported by this segment
of the analysis.

　　Despite this level of support for the hypothesized linkages, four
of the variables that were expected to predict recidivism (and that
have done so in some previous studies) have low and statistically nonsignificant associations with the recidivism variable: race, sex,
family situation, and socioeconomic status. Race does approach the
preset .05 significance level, but the level of the association (Yule's
$Q = -.094$) is obviously weak; and the difference between the recidivism

---

　　*Yule's Q is a measure of the degree of association that exists
between two dichotomized variables; gamma is essentially an extension
of Q to the somewhat more complex problems involved in gauging the
association between ordered variables when one or both variables is
a polytomy. Both may be interpreted as the proportion of improvement in predictions that is obtained beyond chance when the ordering
of pairs of observations are taken into consideration.

　　[†]The fact that there is a relationship between offense type, offense record, and type of information that is made a matter of official
record has already been noted. That bias becomes obvious when these
rates of recidivism are examined. For example, information on school
attendance is most frequently obtained when the court orders a background investigation on a juvenile whose offense and/or offense record
are defined as relatively serious. Thus, the rate of recidivism is
greater than the overall rate in the entire sample for both those who
are in school (40.5) and those who are not (52.2). An adjustment for
the bias created by the missing data is described later in the chapter.
The point that should be noted here is that many common methods of
estimating values for missing data (for example, using the mean or
median of the distribution observed for the valid cases as an "unbiased
estimate" of what the value of missing cases would have most probably
been) are totally inappropriate when systematic biases of this type
contribute substantially to the volume of missing data.

rate of black juveniles (31.2) is only slightly greater than that of whites (27.3). Similarly, the variation in rates between males (29.6) and females (26.4) is not great, nor is that which is noted between those from intact homes (37.6) and those from disrupted homes (40.4). Perhaps the most surprising nonsignificant association is that noted between socioeconomic status and recidivism; the data failed to reveal any significant differences in rates of recidivism unless the rate among those from the highest socioeconomic category (29.0) is compared with that of the lowest of the five categories (35.3).

Shifting attention from the uncontrolled analysis to the conditional associations that were calculated after time at risk was held constant, some interesting changes, as anticipated, can be noted. First, the recidivism rates among each grouping with a longer risk period is higher than that for the same grouping that was exposed to a shorter risk period. Thus, for example, although the level of association between the codefendant variable and recidivism is roughly the same (Yule's Q = -0.337 for the low risk group; -0.320 for those in the high risk category), the rate of recidivism among those in the low risk group who had no codefendants (30.5) is a good deal lower than that noted for the same group who had a longer risk period (48.2). Indeed, to pursue this example just one step further, the recidivism rate among the high risk cohort who did have codefendants (32.5) is slightly higher than that found for the low risk group who did not have codefendants (30.5).

Equally if not more important, however, is the finding that variables that serve as significant overall predictors of recidivism are not necessarily equally good or even significant predictors when the risk period is held constant. As can be seen in Table 7.2, these differences are more apparent under the high-risk condition than under low risk. Under the low-risk condition, every predictor variable that was significantly associated with recidivism under the uncontrolled condition remains significant. Moreover, in five of the seven cases involving significant initial associations, the magnitude of the conditional association actually increased. Second, under the high-risk condition, the religious activity variable became insignificantly associated with recidivism, the magnitude of the association with age was considerably reduced (from -0.392 to -0.193); and, overall, in five of the seven comparisons the conditional associations are of less magnitude than the initial associations. Thus, it would appear that the quality of the predictions of recidivism that can be obtained by taking each individual predictor variable into consideration are reduced as the period of risk increases and as the influences of unmeasured variables are felt.

Until this point in the analysis, attention has been focused on which variables under examination facilitated the prediction of recidi-

vism and the extent to which the quality of predictions obtained varied
when the influence of risk time was held constant. This initial series
of questions having been addressed, the next major task is to determine whether the several predictor variables that were significantly
linked to recidivism can be combined into a single predictor variable
that is capable of accounting for a significant proportion of the variation in recidivism even when the obviously important risk time variable is held constant. There are several ways to approach this task,
perhaps the most frequent way in recent studies being predictive attribute analysis.

Predictive attribute analysis suffers from at least two shortcomings, however, even when the size of the sample being analyzed
is large. First, in its most typical form all variables must be dichotomized. This wastes information provided by measurements at
or above the level of nominal scales and ignores nonlinear trends
that might be revealed by such alternative methods as more sophisticated regression models. Second, as anyone who has ever had the
misfortune to rely on official records data can quickly attest to,
those assigned the task of collecting records data are not among the
most meticulous people in the world, nor are they invariably sensitive to the needs of behavioral science researchers. Thus, missing
data are more often the rule than the exception. This, in turn, creates serious problems in the application of the predictive attribute
analysis technique.

The virtues and liabilities of alternative methods of analysis
notwithstanding, several problems, particularly the one presented by
a high proportion of missing data on several of the predictor variables
for which data are not systematically obtained unless a background investigation is ordered by the court, demanded that some option to
more standard methods be employed in this study. The desired measure was computed in the following manner. First, the initial levels
of association between the predictor variables and recidivism were
examined. Those with insignificant associations with recidivism were
excluded from consideration. Second, each of the relevant contingency
tables were examined to obtain three types of information: the simple
probability of recidivism, the conditional probability of recidivism
for each category of the predictor variable, and the conditional probability of recidivism for those cases for whom data on the predictor
variable was missing. A weight was then computed by calculating a
ratio in which the conditional probability was the numerator and the
simple probability was the denominator. Thus, a weight of "1" indicated that the probability that an individual who had a particular attribute would recidivate was neither higher nor lower than chance; a
weight of less than unity indicated that the presence of the trait de-
pressed the probability of recidivism to a level lower than chance; and

a weight of greater than unity indicated a probability of recidivism greater than chance.* Once the appropriate weights for each category of each variable were computed in this fashion, each juvenile was assigned a recidivism prediction score that was equal to the summation of the weights calculated for each of the predictor variables. The lower the value of the prediction measure the lower the predicted rate of recidivism. The range of the values obtained on this composite variable was from 3.63 to 15.36; the median of the distribution was 9.36. The distribution on the prediction scores was then divided into five categories, each of which included roughly 20 percent of the cases and correlated with recidivism.

As can readily be seen from the information presented in Table 7.3, the composite variable is strongly associated with recidivism (gamma = .551). Recall that the probability of recidivism in the total sample was 28.7 per hundred cases. Those with the lowest prediction scores show a considerably lower recidivism rate (only 7.5 per hundred), and those in the highest risk category show a much greater probability of recidivism (53.1 per hundred appearances). Thus, the composite variable appears to categorize those in our sample quite efficiently. Still, because of the previously demonstrated significance of the amount of time that the juveniles were at risk, it is important to control for this potential bias. When time at risk is held constant, however, the magnitude of the association between recidivism prediction scores and actual recidivism remains strong under conditions both of high risk (gamma = .548) and low risk (gamma = .509).

---

*The manner in which these computations were calculated on the school attendance variable provides a clear illustration of both the weighting procedure and the need for determining an unbiased estimate for missing data. An examination of the appropriate contingency table shows that 45.9 percent of the sample (N = 782) were in school, 9.2 percent were not in school (N = 157), and no data on the school status on the remaining 44.8 percent were recorded (N = 763). The recidivism rates on these three groups is 40.5, 52.2, and 11.7. The rate of recidivism for the entire sample is 28.7. This illustrates the point that the mere presence of this particular bit of information is significant: those for whom no data were recorded are significantly less likely to recidivate. The weights for the recidivism prediction socre were then computed by dividing each of these three conditional probabilities by the simple probability of recidivism (28.7). Thus, those in school were assigned a weight of 1.411; those who had dropped out of school a weight of 1.819; and those for whom no school attendance was recorded a weight of .408.

TABLE 7.3

Recidivism by Recidivism Risk
(N = 1,702)

Recidivism	Recidivism Risk				
	Low				High
No	92.5	84.1	72.5	61.4	46.9
	(320)	(284)	(232)	(213)	(164)
Yes	7.5	15.9	27.5	38.6	53.1
	(26)	(54)	(88)	(134)	(186)
Total	100.0	100.0	100.0	100.0	100.0
	(346)	(339)	(320)	(347)	(350)

Note: Gamma = .551; x^2 = 226.57; df = 4; a = .002.

Source: Compiled by the author.

At this point the analysis has shown that many of the hypothetical correlates of recidivism are, in fact, significant predictors of
reappearance, that the insertion of time at risk as a control variable
alters the quality of the predictions obtained, and that it is both possible and useful to merge the significant predictors of recidivism into a
single composite measure that has been termed a recidivism prediction score. The only remaining analytical task is an exploration of
the relative importance of the predictor variables. To do so, a series of stepwise multiple regression equations were computed: one
for an assessment of the importance of each predictor variable when
time at risk was not held constant; one for each category of the dichotomized risk time variable. The magnitude of the standardized
regression coefficients was employed as an estimate of the relative
importance of the predictor variables. In each case the values of the
predictor variables were set equal to the ratios of simple to conditional probabilities used to construct the recidivism prediction scores.
As is illustrated by the material presented in Table 7.4., and as our
earlier discussion implied, race, sex, and socioeconomic status have
a generally insignificant influence on recidivism. To a somewhat
lesser extent, the same can be said with regard to the importance of
family situation, the presence or absence of codefendants, and the
type of disposition received. The most consistently influential variables appear to be offense type, level of religious activity, age at first
offense, and school attendance. Two basic qualifications should, how-

TABLE 7.4

Standardized Regression Coefficients for Predictors of Recidivism
with and without Risk Time as a Control Variable

Variable	Overall (β)	Low–Risk Condition (β)	High–Risk Condition (β)
Age	.163	.173	.078
Race	−.010[a]	−.080	.043[a]
Sex	.033[a]	.016[a]	.047[a]
Socioeconomic	.011[a]	—[b]	.009[a]
Home	.048	.016[a]	.082
School	.111	.087	.146
School behavior	.093	.031	.112
Religious activity	.144	.185	.119
Codefendants	−.069	−.055	−.040[a]
Offense	.111	.116	.106
Disposition	−.045	−.021	−.072

[a]The regression coefficients produced an F ratio not significant
at the .01 level.

[b]The effect of socioeconomic status was too insignificant to warrant its inclusion in the regression equation.

Source: Compiled by the author.

ever, be noted. First, the stepwise procedure represents a technique for arriving at a least–squares solution by taking the best predictor variable into the equation first, then the next best predictor
variable as measured by the variable that has the greatest impact after the initial variable has accounted for some proportion of the variance in the dependent variable, and so on. An alternative method that
altered the order of inclusion of predictor variables would not change
the magnitude of the multiple correlation coefficient but would change
the size of the standardized regression coefficients. Second, even
though the presence of a dichotomized dependent variable suggests
that the level of multiple correlation will be somewhat lower than what
might be expected were this not the case, the multiple correlation coefficients obtained in this segment of the analysis are only moderate
(the overall multiple correlation was 0.428; in the low–risk situation
the coefficient reduces to 0.381; in the high–risk situation it is 0.429).

SUMMARY AND CONCLUSIONS

The purpose of the analysis presented in this chapter has been to assess the extent to which data that are frequently maintained in official juvenile court records can be employed to predict recidivism. Toward that end, attention has been focused on data derived from the official records of a sample of 1,702 juveniles who appeared before two juvenile court jurisdictions one or more times during the period between January 1, 1970, and December 31, 1974.

Several of the findings noted in the analysis merit special mention here. First, it is clear that the amount of time during which a juvenile is eligible to be returned to the juvenile court exerts a very significant influence, both because it clearly alters the probability that recidivism will occur and, more significantly, because it alters the relative importance of variables that have traditionally been employed as predictors of recidivism. For example, the regression analysis shows that school attendance is the most important predictor variable when the analysis focuses only on that segment of the sample that had an above the median time at risk (beta = 0.146), but the same variable is not nearly so important when those with less than the median risk period are examined (beta = 0.087). Second, despite the frequent relevance of such social characteristics as race, sex, and socioeconomic status in much criminological research, these variables appear to play a very insignificant role in the determination of recidivism. The only immediate interpretation of this finding is that the screening process that is obviously manifested in, for example, the decision to arrest and the decision to file a formal petition is sufficiently selective that the importance of such variables is minimized when attention is directed toward the selective group of juveniles whose alleged misconduct results in a formal court appearance.

Finally, and unfortunately, the moderate magnitude of the multiple correlations reported in the analysis clearly underscores the fact that general social background and offense characteristics provide a highly imperfect means of predicting who will and will not return to the juvenile court because of additional delinquent involvement. This, in turn, brings the need for longitudinal studies that measure the impact of influences not a matter of official record, particularly those whose effect is not manifest until after the initial court appearance, into sharp relief. As noted previously, this is one of the major goals of the larger project for which the data reported in this chapter were collected. It is hoped that the analysis of data presently being collected will allow the resolution of some of the questions that are beyond the limits of the data now available. Regardless, it is essential that subsequent studies of recidivism move toward the establishment of conceptual models and the collection of data that will facilitate reductions in the rather substantial proportions of unexplained variation in recidivism described in both this and previous analyses.

REFERENCES

Arbuckle, D. S., and L. Litwack. 1960. "A Study of Recidivism Among Juvenile Delinquents." Federal Probation 24 (December): 45–48.

Baer, D. J. 1970. "Taxonomic Classification of Male Delinquents from Autobiographical Data and Subsequent Recidivism." Journal of Psychology 76 (September): 27–31.

Buikhuisen, W., and H. A. Hoekstra. 1974. "Factors Related to Recidivism." British Journal of Criminology 14 (January): 63–69.

Cockett, R. 1967. "Borstal Training: A Follow–up Study." British Journal of Criminology 7 (April): 150–83.

Eysenck, S. B., and H. J. Eysenck. 1974. "Personality and Recidivism in Borstal Boys." British Journal of Criminology 14 (December): 385–87.

Ferster, E. Z., and T. F. Courtless. 1972. "Post-Disposition Treatment and Recidivism in the Juvenile Court: Towards Justice for All." Journal of Family Law 11 (December): 683–709.

Hawkins, R., and G. Tiedeman. 1975. The Creation of Deviance. Columbus, Ohio: Charles E. Merrill.

Hollingshead, August. 1958. Social Class and Mental Illness. New York: Wiley.

Hutcheson, B. R. et al. 1966. "A Prognostic Predictive Classification of Juvenile Court First Offenders Based on a Follow-up Study." British Journal of Criminology 6 (October): 354-63.

Knight, B. J., and D. J. West. 1975. "Temporary and Continuing Delinquency." British Journal of Criminology 15 (January): 43–50.

Kraus, J. 1970. "Probation as a 'Learning' Experience in Seven Groups of Male Juvenile Delinquents." Australian and New Zealand Journal of Criminology 3 (March): 7-29.

_____. 1973a. "The Response of Male Juvenile Offenders to Court
Caution." Australian and New Zealand Journal of Criminology
6 (June): 75-82.

_____. 1973b. "Judicial Labels as a Typology of Offenses Committed
by Male Juveniles." British Journal of Criminology 13 (July):
269-74.

Kraus, J., and J. Smith. 1973. "The Relationship of Four Types of
'Broken Home' to Some Neglected Parameters of Juvenile Delinquency." Australian Journal of Social Issues 8 (March): 52-
57.

Laulicht, J. 1962. "A Study of Recidivism in One Training School:
Implications for Rehabilitative Programs." Crime and Delinquency 8 (April): 161-71.

_____. 1963. "Problems of Statistical Research: Recidivism and
Its Correlates." Journal of Criminal Law, Criminology, and
Police Science 54 (June): 163-74.

Little, A. 1965. "Parental Deprivation, Separation and Crime: A
Test of Adolescent Recidivism." British Journal of Criminology
5 (October): 419-30.

Mannheim, H., and L. T. Wilkins. 1955. Prediction Methods in
Relation to Borstal Training. London: Her Majesty's Stationery
Office.

Meade, A. 1973. "Seriousness of Delinquency, the Adjudication Decision and Recidivism—a Longitudinal Configurational Analysis."
Journal of Criminal Law and Criminology 64 (December): 478-85.

Miller, S. J., and S. Dinitz. 1973. "Measuring Institutional Impact."
Criminology 11 (September): 417-26.

Rosenberg, J. P. 1973. "Female Juvenile Delinquency: A Nineteenth-
Century Follow-up." Crime and Delinquency 19 (March): 72-78.

Scott, P. D. 1964. "Approved School Success Rates." British Journal of Criminology 4 (October): 525-46.

Sepsi, V. J., Jr. 1974. "Girl Recidivists." Journal of Research in
Crime and Delinquency 11 (March): 70-79.

Tannenbaum, Frank. 1938. Crime and Community. New York: Ginn.

Thomas, C. W., and R. J. Cage. 1975. "The Effect of Social Characteristics on Juvenile Court Dispositions." Paper presented
   to the Southern Sociological Association, Washington, D. C.

Thomas, C. W., G. A. Kreps, and R. J. Cage. 1975. "The Appli-
   cation of Compliance Theory to the Study of Juvenile Delinquency."
   Paper presented to the Midwest Sociological Society, Chicago,
   Ill.

Thomas, C. W., and J. S. Williams. 1974. "The Deterrent Effect
   of Sanctions: A Selected Bibliography." Williamsburg, Va.:
   Metropolitan Criminal Justice Center.

Thornberry, T. P. 1971. "Punishment and Crime: The Effect of
   Legal Dispositions on Subsequent Criminal Behavior." Ph. D.
   dissertation, University of Pennsylvania.

Unkovic, C. M., and W. J. Ducsay. 1969. "An Application of Con-
   figural Analysis to the Recidivism of Juvenile Delinquent Behavior." Journal of Criminal Law, Criminology, and Police
   Science 60 (December): 340-44.

Uusitalo, P. 1972. "Recidivism after Release from Closed and Open
   Penal Institutions." British Journal of Criminology 12 (September): 221-29.

8

HIDDEN DELINQUENCY AND
JUDICIAL SELECTION
IN BELGIUM
Josine Junger-Tas

THEORETICAL CONSIDERATIONS

Why a Hidden Delinquency Study?

For a long time criminologists have thought that the real object of their scientific endeavors was the criminal, as he was caught, judged, and defined by society. While as early as the nineteenth century some of them expressed doubts about the reliability of official statistics (McClintock, 1970), research was long limited to recorded criminality. More recently, however, two fundamental problems have been raised:

Do official statistics reflect—or are they representative of—all committed offenses?

Are prosecuted offenders representative of the total offender population?

Studying the first problem, researchers found several factors affecting the recording of an offense. One is its seriousness. Erickson and Empey (1963), interviewing 15- to 17-year-old boys, found that, though nine out of ten less serious offenses (property destruction, traffic violations) were not discovered, even eight out of ten serious offenses (car theft) were not detected. Department stores rarely report detected shoplifting to the police, considering this as a working expense. Victims do not always report offenses to the police for a variety of reasons: shame or fear (sex offenses); the victim and offender may be the same (abortion, drug abuse); doubts about police effectiveness; or unwillingness to get involved with the police (Ennis,

1973). Finally, prosecuting practices also affect official statistics; a rise or a decline in drug abuse rates can be the simple result of changing prosecuting emphasis.

The second problem has been studied mainly by comparing registered (and/or institutionalized) offenders with boys who admit having committed offenses. The comparison resulted in the reconsideration of some important variables traditionally associated with delinquency. One of the most notable findings in this respect was that there is only a slight, if any, relationship between social class and delinquent behavior. This finding casts doubt on the subcultural theoretical approach whose basic assumption is that of a strong relationship between lower social class and delinquency (Merton, 1957; Cohen, 1960; Cloward and Ohlin, 1960). Other traditional variables supported by the use of such comparisons are the broken family and the working mother. Short and Nye (1957) found that half of their training school population came from a broken family, while only a fourth of high school boys reporting offenses did. The relation of the working mother with delinquent behavior appeared to be spurious (Hirschi, 1972).

Sex and age differences did persist, however, whatever method of data collection was used (Short and Nye, 1957; Gold, 1970, Van Bostraeten, 1974; Jongman and Smale, 1972). A Belgian study showed that children, mostly males, referred to the juvenile court were between 15 and 18 years old (Junger-Tas, 1971). Research by the self-report method gave comparable results (Gold, 1970), whereas a Dutch study among university students showed that delinquency declined steadily after age 18 (Buikhuisen et al., 1969).

Nevertheless, it seems clear that recorded delinquency is heavily biased; it gives no clear picture of the extent and nature of delinquent behavior, nor of the offender population. To gain a better insight into these two basic questions, we decided to study a representative sample of an urban youth population of 15- to 18-year-old youths, girls as well as boys, students as well as working youths, Belgian as well as children of guest workers.

Judicial Selection Process

If differences between recorded delinquency and self-reported delinquency are as substantial as suspected, the conclusion that some selection process takes place is inevitable. The real problem is what criteria are used in this selection process. The emphasis placed, in most Western countries, on the idea of protecting the young "for their own good" against living conditions that could harm them, leads to the situation that the offense is not the main element determining judicial action. Other criteria become more important, centering around the question: Is this child in "physical or moral danger," does he need protection? (Belgian law). The trouble is that most of the variables affecting official action are unknown or unclear. However, some research results are available. A first question concerns the risk of being caught by the police. Gold (1920) found that frequency of delinquent behavior was related to getting caught. Others concluded that, though many young people commit offenses, official delinquents commit more serious offenses and do so more often (Murphy et al., 1969). Erickson and Empey (1963) found that repeated offenders run a greater risk of being caught than one-time offenders. Police practice is also a factor. There are some, mainly American, studies about police decisions. Piliavin and Briar (1964), observing police contacts with juveniles, concluded that the most important decision criteria are previous contact with the police, appearance, and behavior. Goldman (1963) added other criteria for differential selection of juveniles: appreciation of the offense; police attitudes toward the offender and his family and toward juvenile court; police views about their own role and about community expectations. A study of decision making on the basis of information showed two elements to be decisive: nature of the offense and behavior of the offender (Sullivan and Siegel, 1972). Observing practices of the police, Cicourel (1968) emphasized how much they categorize juveniles according to broken homes, "bad attitudes" toward authority, poor school performance, ethnic origins, low-income families, thus contributing to the definition of what delinquency "really" is.

A second important level of decision making is that of the prosecutor. The prosecutor's decisions remain uncontrolled. Since his main objective is "to protect children whose health, security or morality is in danger" (Belgian law), one might expect all views and prejudices prevalent in society to affect his decision. A Dutch study of dismissal policy found a relationship with social class: charges against working-class juveniles were less frequently dismissed (Jongman and Smale, 1972). Still, all researchers do not agree. Shannon (1963) made a study of the relation between the number of referrals and the number of police contacts. He suggested that the greater number of court referrals in lower-class areas is related to the nature and pattern of offenses and does not express discrimination. Terry (1967) concluded that whatever differences existed in decisions about juveniles, they disappeared on introduction of control variables.

Summarizing the findings we must admit that they are not conclusive: although there are strong indicators that some selection takes place, the criteria used are not very clear. The second objective of our study was, therefore, to clarify some of the mechanisms that operate to constitute the officially labeled delinquent population.

Background of Delinquent Behavior

In this study delinquency will not be considered as an attribute of a juvenile, but as an ordinal variable. Delinquent behavior is defined by committing one or more acts that would be considered offenses if committed by an adult.

In a previous longitudinal study among referred delinquents, we have stressed the concept of social integration. The general idea was that, if juvenile delinquents were to succeed in integrating well in important social subsystems, they would give up delinquent behavior. This hypothesis has been confirmed. A sample of 88 boys has been studied with respect to social integration and recidivism three years after their appearance before court: 51 of them (58 percent) had no other contacts with court or police; 23 of them had contacts with police only, and 14 boys were reconvicted (Buikhuisen et al., 1969). This approach can be summarized by stating that the more a person is integrated in conventional society, the less he will be inclined to transgress legal norms. Comparable views have been developed by social control theorists (Nye, 1958; Matza, 1964; Reckless, 1961; Hirschi, 1972). The social integration concept includes four important elements or criteria.

1. Close ties with significant others. This element is stressed by many researchers. Matza as well as Nye insisted on the role of parents in achieving norm-respecting behavior. According to Matza, as parents represent conventional order, close ties with them insulate children from deviant behavior. Nye stresses direct and indirect control by parents, to achieve interiorization of conventional norms. For Hirschi the crucial element is attachment to parents and to other significant persons, such as teachers or friends. Reckless, speaking about outer containment, mentions "acceptance, identity and belongingness."

2. Desire to conform, to commit oneself to conventional systems, to project oneself in the future in a conforming way. Reckless sees this as "goal-orientation" combined with "a reasonable set of social expectations." Hirschi and Matza call this element "commitment to the conventional order."

3. Good social functioning in relevant subsystems. This is emphasized by Hirschi as "involvement in conventional activities."

4. Adoption of the general value pattern and social norms and respect for legal norms.

Most control theorists agree on these points. We prefer the term social integration because social control has some negative connotations, whereas we want to stress the positive rewards related to integration. One obeys the law not only because of the risks of being caught but also because of what one gains by it.

The hypotheses we examined with respect to delinquent behavior of adolescents are as follows:

1. The closer relations with significant others, the less delinquent behavior;

2. The greater the desire to conform and to commit oneself in conventional systems, the less delinquent behavior;

3. The more social functioning in these systems meets conventional expectations, the less delinquent behavior;

4. The more certain general and some specific values and norms are respected, the less delinquent behavior.

DESIGN OF THE STUDY

The Sample

A relatively small urban community, part of a big city, was selected for the study. Its mainly working-class population included 31 percent foreigners, mostly South European, North African, and Turkish. The total youth population of 15- to 18-year-olds numbered 790 juveniles: 40 had been interviewed during a pilot study, 132 no longer lived at the given address; so 618 juveniles were effectively approached. The interviewing took four months, during which 65 percent of this group, or 402 interviews, were completed. Only 8 percent refused; 3 percent did not speak French; 24 percent could not be interviewed: some worked at irregular hours, some were doing their military service, but most of them simply were never at home when the interviewer came, or did not keep their appointments. We might have reduced this number, but we did not want to extend the interviewing period because too many juveniles would then be informed about the study.

How representative is the sample? This was checked for sex, age, and nationality. Concerning sex and nationality the sample is quite representative. Regarding age distribution, such is not the case: the 15-year-olds are underrepresented, and the 17-year-olds are overrepresented (for some characteristics of the sample, see Table 8.1). However, as neither the introductory letter nor the interviewer's introduction mentioned the subject delinquency, we do not think that actual delinquents are underrepresented among those interviewed.

TABLE 8.1

Some Characteristics of the Sample

	Percentage
Sex	
Boys	52.5
Girls	47.5
Age	
15–16	13.5
16–17	35.5
17–18	51
Nationality groups	
Belgians	63
South Europeans	17.5
North Africans (plus Turks)	17
More than four children per family	
Belgians	27.5
South Europeans	39
North Africans	70

Source: Compiled by the author.

The Interview

Introductory letters were written to all youngsters asking for their participation. The interviewers (mostly students) used a structured, precoded interview schedule that included some open questions to get specifications about certain points. Interviewers received a special training, and much emphasis was placed on the introduction to questions about delinquent acts.

Delinquency Measures

Questions were asked about 17 offenses: seven acts against property, four aggressive acts, three traffic violations, two acts of drug abuse and one falsifying an identity paper. Truancy, running away from home, and trouble with parents, though included in the interview schedule, were not considered as delinquency. Four measures were devised. The first measured the number of different acts committed; the second measured the frequency (once; two or three times;

four or more times); the third measured the seriousness, by a score
running from one to five. The seriousness score was the result of a
special study among 425 young people: university students, technical
students, high school students, and working youngsters. They were
asked to grade each offense on a ten-point scale with respect to seriousness. Resulting classifications were compared with respect to age,
sex, education, social status: correlations were all highly significant.
Finally, a fourth measure combined the others to form a delinquency
index. Correlations between measures range from .92 to .97.

Reliability and Validity

Great care was given to reliability and validity. A pilot study
was undertaken to test out the interview schedule. Interviewers were
carefully trained. Their freedom of manipulation was restricted,
while theory and hypotheses were not communicated. Foreigners
were interviewed by their own countrymen, which proved particularly
important with respect to North African respondents. All this and the
preliminary letter were designed to minimize possible apprehension
about participation, which might affect validity. A partial check of
validity consisted of comparing police records with self-reported offenses, and with the mentioning of having been picked up by the police.
On this basis, we can infer a reasonable validity of about 75 percent.
Of course the self-report method has its drawbacks, of which the
validity problem is a major one. Trust in the method could come
partly from the consistency of overall results in different parts of the
world. Another solution is to consider results as broad tendencies
rather than as absolute truths.

Analysis of Results

Most of the analyses were done by computer techniques. Simple univariate analysis was done using the lambda^2 and the Mann
Whitney tests. But multivariate techniques, such as analysis of variance and multiple regression analysis, were also used. Additional
information on open questions was analyzed manually.

RESULTS

Extent and Nature of Delinquency

As Christie (1965) rightly remarks, every list of items is a
selection out of the universum of possible offenses. We selected ours
on the basis of police reports and discussions with juveniles.

TABLE 8.2

Selected Offenses and Percent of Respondents Reporting Them
(N = 270)

Offense	Percentage
Breaking and entering	37
Shoplifting	34
Stealing at school	32
Consuming without paying	22
Stealing money	22
Stealing bicycle, motorbicycle (or car: 4)	12
Assault	21
Threatening with assault	21
Property destruction (plus arson: 5)	20
Driving a motorbicycle permanently at too high speed	24.5
Driving without insurance	17
Driving when drunk	9
Drug use	8
Falsifying identity card	7

Source: Compiled by the author.

The percentages in Table 8.2 are calculated on those who have
reported at least one offense, that is two-thirds of the sample. Thirty-
nine percent of the sample reported one or two acts, 28.5 percent reported three or more, and 12 percent reported five or more. The
data show that most of the delinquent acts are offenses against property. Acts against property and traffic violations seem to be committed
more frequently than aggressive acts: 54.5 percent of the traffic
violations and 30 percent of the acts against property occurred four
times or more, compared with 18 percent of aggressive offenses
$(p < 0.001)$.

Comparison with other studies is difficult. First, research
populations differ; Christie (1965) and Anttila (1966) studied recruits;
Buikhuisen (1969) studied university students; Nye (1958), Gold (1970),
and Elmhorn (1965) used samples of schoolchildren. Second, every
study made a different selection of offenses; for example, Gold's list
included truancy, running away, violence against parents, and sexual
relations, most of which we included but did not consider as delinquency.
Finally, the number of items also affects results. Our collective conclusion could perhaps be that the fact of committing one or two delinquent acts during adolescence is statistically normal. But it should

be stressed that 73 percent of the offenders reported 47 percent of all the committed acts, whereas 53 percent of those acts were reported by only 27 percent of the offenders. So, a little more than a fourth of the offenders claims to be responsible for more than half of the offenses.

Is Delinquent Behavior a Group Activity?

— Many theorists seem to think that delinquency is a group activity (Cohen, 1960; Cloward and Ohlin, 1960; Miller, 1972). However, empirical research has had difficulty locating well-structured gangs (Short and Strodtbeck, 1965; Yablonski, 1962). Most researchers agree that there are only loosely knit groups with changing membership (Yablonski's near-groups). In this respect our data are somewhat surprising: 43.5 percent of the offenses were committed alone; 35.5 percent in company of some friends; and only 21 percent were group activities. Thus, when not committed alone, most offenses were committed with one or two peers. But much depends on the nature of the act. Sixty-three percent of the following acts were solitary enterprises: stealing at school, stealing money, violence against persons, threatening, and all traffic violations. Acts that are mostly (77 percent) committed in company of others are breaking and entering, shoplifting, property destruction, drug use.

Sex and Delinquent Behavior

Delinquency of women and girls is a much neglected research area. In many cases the researcher is satisfied with stating that criminality of women is less than that of men and mostly restricted to sexual offenses. Belgian statistics on youth protection show that the ratio of boys to girls is three to one on the prosecuting level, and two to one on court level. Officially, girls' delinquency is mainly running away from home, incorrigibility, and premature sexual relations. What does self-reported delinquency show? Boys report more acts than do girls: 44.5 percent of the girls, against 21.5 percent of the boys, reported no offenses. The mean number of reported acts by boys is 2.53, by girls is 1.28, a very significant difference. The same is true for frequency and seriousness. Therefore, it can be said that the delinquency of boys is more extended, more frequent, and more serious than for girls. However, differences are not quite as large as official statistics suggest. Of every hundred boys, 79 reported at least one offense; of every hundred girls, 56 did. This brings the ratio of boys to girls to 1.4 to 1. With respect to the na-

TABLE 8.3

Sex Differences for Selected Family and School Variables
(in percent)

	Boys (N = 210)	Girls (N = 189)	p Values - λ^2
Parents know youth's friends	60	80.5	p < .05
Parents tell youth when to be home	59.5	76	p < .001
Youth spends leisure mostly at home	24	49	p < .001
Quarrels often with mother	14	29	p < .01
Quarrels often with father	15	22	*
Goes out with parents or one good friend	10.5	22	p < .001
Likes very much to go to school	54	68.5	p < .02
Spends more than one-half hour per day on schoolwork	26.5	46	p < .110
Discipline index 5 or more	40	29	p < .12
Played truant 5 times or more	54.5	35	p < .05

*Not significant.

Source: Compiled by the author.

ture of the offense, no difference could be found concerning acts
against property, drug use, and falsifying identification cards, but
girls reported significantly less aggressive acts and traffic violations.
Examining two traditional variables supposed to be related to the de-
linquncy of girls, running away and premature sexual relations, our
data show that girls do not run away from home more often than boys
(11 percent versus 12 percent), nor do they report more sexual relations (24 percent versus 35 percent, though there may be some under-
reporting here). So, contrary to expectations, many girls report offenses; and their delinquency is much like that of boys. In line with
our theoretical assumptions, we hypothesized that the major reason
for differences in delinquent behavior between girls and boys would
be the greater social control exercised on girls. This was checked
for some family and school variables (Table 8.3). Differences are
nearly all significant and in the expected direction; parents do indeed

control their daughters more than they do their sons. Nearly half the girls and only a fourth of the boys spend their free time at home. When girls go out they do this more often with parents or one good friend. At school girls are less often punished, they play truant less often, and they spend more time at their homework. Curiously, they quarrel more with their parents, probably as a result of their greater closeness to them.

Social Class and Delinquency

Our data confirm what researchers all over the world have found: there is no relation whatsoever between social class and delinquent behavior. Analysis of variance on the four delinquency measures showed no difference between the six status categories. Analysis of each offense did not produce any difference either. However, two corrections have to be made. Social status of juveniles themselves, as determined by going to school or working already (instead of occupation of father), is related to the frequency and seriousness of offenses. The mean delinquency index of school-going respondents is 9.03, for working ones it is 12.35 (F = 4.47, p < .05). These differences do not disappear when the occupation of father is held constant. In the case of nationality held constant, they remain very significant for Belgian respondents, are somewhat less for South Europeans, and hardly exist at all for North Africans.

The second correction concerns nature of the offense. Empirical research has shown a relation between social class and aggressive delinquency. Miller (1966) found that the lower the social status, the more violence. Middle-class gangs were characterized by the absence of violence (Muerhoff, 1967). Dutch research also found more violence in the lower social classes (Jongman, 1971). To test this, we selected, from the offender group, two subgroups presenting a pronounced property offense pattern or aggressive-offensive pattern. * Comparing them, it appeared that only 3 percent of aggressive offenders came from highest status groups, against 22 percent of property offenders; 36.5 percent against 22 percent came from the lowest. Another index of social class, education, was also significantly related to nature of the offense: aggressive offenders were more often technical school students; property offenders were more often high school or college students.

_____

*This means that the distribution of the reported acts was heavily biased in the direction of violence or property.

Nationality and Delinquency

Children of guest workers reported considerably fewer offenses than Belgian children. The mean number of offenses for Belgian, South European, and North African (including Turkish) juveniles was, respectively, 2.20, 1.76, and 1.08 (F = 6.69, p < .01). Many European studies—mostly on recorded criminality—gave comparable results. A Belgian study on Italian guest workers of 16 to 25 years of age found little criminality, but more violence (Liben, 1963). A Swiss study noted that criminality of foreigners is highest among Austrians, followed by Germans, Italians, Arabs, and Turks (Graven, 1965). Kaiser (1971) remarks for Germany that, if German male criminality is 100, criminality of Turks is 88, of Greeks 72, of Italians 50, and of Spaniards 32.

Our data confirm this picture; compared with Belgian juveniles, children of guest workers report less delinquent acts, but more aggressive acts (Table 8.4). Now, why is this so? A well-known hypothesis of Sellin (1938) attributes criminality of immigrants essentially to frictions between different culture patterns. However, this hypothesis does not seem very probable in the case of guest workers. Though specific culture-bound criminality does exist, it is only a very small part of total delinquency. Moreover, if the hypothesis is correct, one would expect more delinquency among those who are newly arrived in Belgium. This is not so. The longer foreigners live in Belgium, the more their delinquency approaches the Belgian pattern. Differences in the number of reported acts between Belgian and South European juveniles are not as large as those between Belgian and North African juveniles (Table 8.5).

TABLE 8.4

Social Class and Mean Number of Reported Offenses and
Delinquency Index
(N = 344)

	Mean Number of Offenses	Mean Delinquency Index
Highest social status 1	1.9	9.24
2	2.4	12.09
3	2.1	10.13
4	1.7	9.34
5	2.1	11.58
Lowest social status 6	1.4	7.84

Source: Compiled by the author.

TABLE 8.5

Proportions of Belgians and Foreigners Reporting Offenses

	Belgians (N = 191)	Foreigners (N = 79)	p Values
Breaking and entering	39.5	30.5	*
Shoplifting	37	24	p < .05
Stealing in school	35.5	23	p < .05
Consuming without paying	26	14	p < .01
Stealing money	22	21.5	*
Stealing bicycle/motorcycle	10	15	*
Assault	18	28	p < .05
Threatening with assault	16	33	p < .01
Property destruction	20.5	15	*
Permanent too high speed on motorcycle	28	16.5	p < .05
Driving without insurance	18.5	14	*
Drunken driving	12.5	—	—

*Not significant.

Source: Compiled by the author.

Another hypothesis is based on the central idea that violence as a solution for human problems is a basic value in some subcultural groups (Wolfgang and Ferracuti, 1967). Our data seem to support this hypothesis: those groups that are least adapted to Belgian culture report few delinquent acts, but those that are reported are more aggressive. On the other hand, foreign parents appear to control their children more strictly than Belgian parents; children of guest workers spend their leisure time more often with their family, when parents tell them at what time they have to be home they obey them, and they quarrel much less with them. All this tends to support the violent subculture hypothesis.

Social Integration and Delinquency

The first hypothesis with respect to social integration refers to relations with significant others, such as parents, teachers, boss, friends. Some family variables have traditionally been associated with delinquency. One such variable is the broken family. Though the broken family seems to be a selection criterion for the juvenile court (Short and Nye, 1957), its relation with delinquency—though weaker—persists in the case of self-reported acts. The percentage of juveniles reporting three or more offenses is, among those who have both parents, 25 percent; among those with one parent, 37.5 percent; and among those with a step-parent, 49 percent. The effect of the broken family is the same for boys and girls, leading in both cases to more serious and more frequent delinquent behavior.

Another variable frequently associated with delinquency is the working mother. Our data show no relation between this variable and delinquent behavior (43 percent of the mothers in the sample worked outside the home). Degree of delinquency is not affected by a mother's working, because working mothers are an accepted phenomenon in Belgian society. Employers and schools offer social facilities to guard and supervise children.

Relations with parents were measured by questions about quarreling, talking over problems with them, impartiality of parents, and running away from home (multiple regression coefficient R = .30). Highest contributions came from running away and number of times this happened (partials: + .14, + .13). Three-fourths of the runaways declared they did this after a big fight at home. No clear distinction could be made between effect of father-items and effect of mother-items; both appeared equally important. This seems to contradict much literature on the determining effects of the mother on later behavior (Bowlby, 1952). Does delinquency of children lead to bad relations with parents, or is it the other way around? In studies of official delinquency this question cannot be solved. We found that only 35 percent of the reported acts were known to parents. In most cases youngsters simply told their parents what they had done, but they were careful to talk only about minor acts like traffic violations, entering, and fighting. The frequency and seriousness of most delinquent acts are unknown to parents. Consequently, this behavior cannot influence relations between parents and their offspring. It looks as if it is the other way around: bad relations with parents seem to be causally related to delinquency. Examining six parental control variables (R = .37), we found that the most important were: parents tell respondent at what time to be home; respondent obeys; and the parents' reaction to truancy by the child (partials: + .16, −.25, +.28). The latter variable is positively related to delinquency; the more the parent reacts violently, the more frequent the delinquent behavior. Gold (1970) also notes that parents of delinquents often try to discipline their children, but mostly without success. Relations with school-teachers and their boss showed a weak but consistently negative association with delinquent behavior.

Much theorizing has been devoted to relations with peers. Subcultural theory considers gang delinquency as a solution to a collective

problem; differential association theory states that integration in a
group with a delinquent value system makes one into a delinquent. A
repeated finding in empirical research is that delinquents have delinquent friends. Our study is no exception. We found a zero order correlation of + .45 between the number of friends who had contacts with
police and delinquent behavior. But other factors discriminated between youth with, and youth without, delinquent friends. Those with
delinquent friends had significantly poorer relations with their parents
and a greater autonomy from parental control. This could lead more
easily to association with other marginal youths. However, our data
do not support the hypothesis that delinquents find in their peer group
trust, warmth, affection, or support. We tested this by a number
of questions about expectations from friends, talking about problems,
identification with friends. No difference was found in this respect
between delinquents and nondelinquents (with a weak tendency for delinquents to have less confidence in friends and attach less importance
to friends' opinions).

The second hypothesis stated that commitment to the conventional
system would be related to less delinquent behavior. This was tested
for school and work situations. The most telling variables with respect to school were: liking to go to school (- .13) and time spent on
homework (- .08; R = .17). As to the work situation, some variables
weakly correlate in the expected direction: juveniles who declare
that they work hard and find their work useful and important reported
less offenses than juveniles who did not think so. But the variables
that contributed most are: work aspirations (+ .25) and expectations
about aspirations (- .13). Delinquency is strongly related to general
discontent with the actual work situation. Cloward and Ohlin (1960)
stated that discrepancy between aspirations and expectations, causing
frustrations, produced delinquency. Our data give some support to
this hypothesis: the skilled workers (29 percent) reported less offenses than the unskilled workers (71 percent). However, the question
remains if actual frustrations are attributed to social and cultural
barriers, or to personal inadequacy. Though our data are not conclusive on this point, they indicate that considerably more working
than school-going juveniles played truant, and a large proportion of
them did not finish their education.

According to the third hypothesis, functioning adequately in important social worlds such as school, work, and leisure, insulates
one from delinquency. School variables analyzed were school grades,
truancy, punishment, time spent on homework, and number of classes
repeated. High contributions were given by: frequency of truancy
(+ .25), punishment index (+ .25), and time spent on homework (- .16).
The multiple regression coefficient, R = .44, is higher than the coefficient of relations with—and control by—parents (R = .30 and R = .37).

Do lower-class children repeat classes more often than higher-class children? Our data do not confirm this Cohen (1960) hypothesis: children who repeat class two, three, or four times show exactly the same social distribution as the whole sample. Persistent class repeaters get punished more often, play truant more often, and dislike school much more; all of which are related to delinquency.

Concerning work, only one variable appeared to be really important: job instability (+ .25). This is consistent with the finding that general discontent with one's job is positively related to delinquency, both being typical integration variables. Functioning well in the school and work systems entails important rewards such as appreciation and good relations with teachers and boss. Functioning badly means bad relations and low status. It makes one indifferent to the opinion of others and insensitive to their values and norms. Without rewards one has little to lose by committing offenses. However, as these juveniles grow older, receive some education, have a better paid job, get married and have children, the risks of criminality become greater, they have much more to lose, so inhibitions toward delinquent behavior develop.

Leisure time variables were related to delinquency (R = .51). Most important were spending free time with delinquent friends (+ .39) and spending free time mostly outside the home (+ .22). A frequent feeling of boredom was also related to delinquency (+ .09). Juveniles who go out with a large group or alone report more offenses than juveniles who go out with one good friend or with parents. Subanalysis showed that juveniles who are often bored, who go out in large groups, who spend most of their time outside the home and commit truancy more often, are less committed to school and less attached to parents. We noted that juveniles with delinquent friends show less integration in family, school, and work. The importance of delinquent friends appears also from the fact that 80 percent of the offenses that were discussed with others were discussed with friends. More than half their friends gave no comment at all, while 47 percent reacted favorably. In other words, friends do accept, favor, and encourage illegal behavior.

With respect to the fourth hypothesis, two questions can be raised: are values consistent with behavior, and do values determine behavior, or are they justifications of behavior? This was tested by six items: will respondent bring up his children as he was brought up, has he/she already had sexual relations, could most illegal acts be considered as delinquency, would he commit them if he was sure of not being detected, do the police in general earn respect, and do the police discriminate? The multiple correlation coefficient was .41.

Our first conclusion was that values and behavior are rather consistent. Juveniles who say they would commit offenses if they were

sure of not being caught reported more offenses (+ .31). On the other
hand, the more one respects the police, the less one reports delinquent acts (- .11). Correlation of possible discrimination by the police with delinquency is in the expected direction but much weaker;
most respondents were convinced that the police discriminate on race
and outward appearance (- .05). Having sexual relations under the
age of 18 indicates infringement of an important social norm and considerable autonomy with respect to significant adults (+ .19). A striking fact is that, of those who want to bring up their children just as
they have been brought up, 44 percent report no delinquent act, which
is twice as many as those who do not accept the parental model, or
all parental values. We also tested two values related to school and
work. Juveniles who judge that high school grades or commitment to
work are not important report more offenses than do juveniles who
think high school grades and doing their very best at work are really
important. Pronounced delinquent behavior is consistent with rejecting conventional norms with respect to family, school, work, illegal
behavior, and police intervention. But, perhaps, this rejecting is
simply rationalizing on the lines of Sykes and Matza's (1957) neutralization techniques. Values are transmitted in the first place by significant adults, such as parents, and perhaps teachers. Our data show
that 55 to 60 percent of youngsters who do not obey parents and do not
get along with teachers do not consider illegal acts as delinquency and
would commit offenses if there were no risk of being caught, against
only a fourth of youngsters who do get along with parents and teachers.
On the other hand, we found the inverse relation with respect to delinquent friends. Delinquent friends clearly reduce attachment to conventional values and approve of delinquent behavior, which is consistent with differential association theory. So it appears that weaker integration in conventional society leads to selecting other marginal
friends, who in turn reinforce deviant values and diminish barriers to
delinquency. (See Talble 8.6 for a summary of some important variables related to delinquency.)

Judicial Selection Processes

Two levels of selection are examined. The first level is the
selection of offenders, that is, juveniles known to the police for one
or more of the 17 offenses for which they were interviewed. The second level is the selection of juveniles on the basis of the Belgian Law
on Youth Protection, which distinguishes four grounds of intervention:
(1) incorrigibility (on charge of parents); (2) physical or moral danger; (3) running away; (4) acts qualified as offenses.

What offenses came to the attention of the police? Of 772 delinquent acts, 165 were said to be discovered (20 percent). But only 22

TABLE 8.6

Some Selected Variables and Number of Reported Acts

	Pearson Correlations	Partial Correlation Coefficients	
		Raw	Normalized
Number of friends with police contacts	+ .45	+ .84	+ .32
Work instability	+ .19	+ .28	+ .14
School discipline—index	+ .31	+ .32	+ .23
Number of times truancy	+ .33	+ .16	+ .14
Running away from home	+ .25	+ .81	+ .12
Obeying parents (on time back at home)	− .18	− .13	− .08

Note: R = .58; explained variable = 33 percent.

Source: Compiled by the author.

percent of these acts were known to the police. The most discovered acts were: theft of motor bicycles (44 percent), fighting (52 percent), theft of money (37 percent), threatening with violence (27 percent), shoplifting (27 percent), and arson (26 percent). The police were aware of some breaking and entering, theft of motor bicycles, property destruction. Of a total of 270 offenders, only 31—or 11.5 percent— were known to the police; this number is reduced to 22 (or 8 percent) at the prosecuting level, and to 12 (or 4.5 percent) at court level. Our conclusion: very few offenders are known by the authorities. On the basis of the law on youth protection, 70 respondents—or 17.5 per- cent of the total sample—came to the attention of the police. This number is again reduced to 13 percent at prosecuting level and 5 per- cent at court level.

At this time we will review other selection criteria. The first is the extent of delinquency. Of the offenders known to the police, 61.5 percent reported three or more offenses, compared with 40 per- cent of the other offenders. Of those selected on youth protection grounds, 43 percent reported three or more offenses, compared with only 22.5 percent of the others. With respect to frequency and seri- ousness, we found the same significant differences. This is true not only at the police level but at the prosecuting and court levels as well (Table 8.7). So we may conclude that frequency and seriousness of offenses are indeed important factors for judicial intervention.

TABLE 8.7

Delinquency of Detected Offenders and of Juveniles Selected on Youth Protection Grounds at Different Judicial Levels

	Three or More Delinquent Acts		Seriousness—Extreme Category		Frequency—Extreme Category		Delinquency Index—Extreme Category	
	Number	Percent	Number	Percent	Number	Percent	Number	Percent
Detected offenders								
Police level (N = 31)	19	61.5	16	51.5	15	48.5	11	35.5
Prosecuting level (N = 22)	13	59	11	50	12	54.5	8	36.5
Court level (N = 11)	7	—	5	—	6	—	4	—
Nondetected offenders (N = 239)	95	40	54	22.5	45	19	37	15.5
Selected juveniles								
Police level (N = 39)	17	43	11	28	10	25.5	8	20.5
Prosecuting level (N = 30)	11	37	8	27	7	23.5	6	20
Court level (N = 9)	6	—	3	—	3	—	2	—
Nonselected juveniles (N = 329)	74	22.5	41	12.5	35	11	27	8

Source: Compiled by the author.

With respect to sex, the percentages of girls known for an offense on the three intervention levels are 3, 2, and 2 percent; on the
basis of youth protection selection, the proportions are 11, 85, and
37 percent. Even if one takes into account that boys' delinquency is
more frequent and more serious, there is a considerable bias in favor
of girls.

There also seems to be a bias against North Africans. Of the
total offender group, 70 percent are Belgian, 18.5 percent South European, and 11.5 percent North African. The distribution of offenders
known to the police and at the prosecuting level is quite different: 60
percent Belgian, 13.5 percent South European, but 26.5 percent North
African juveniles. The explanation of this might be that police patrol-
ling and police controls are more frequent in areas with high concen-
trations of immigrant workers, so perception—and selection—of mis-
behavior is probably more extensive. Another reason might be the
more aggressive character of delinquency of North African juveniles.
In the case of selection based on youth protection law, this bias does
not exist.

The broken family does not seem a selection criterion for the
police. But it is a clear selection factor for the court. At the court
level half the offenders as well as half the selected juveniles come
from broken families against about 30 percent at the police level.

Concerning social class, selection is also clearly biased. At
the police level this is not as apparent for juveniles selected on youth
protection grounds as it is for selected offenders. However, the proportion of lower-class juveniles grows at every intervention level.
At the court level there are comparatively twice as many lower-class
juveniles as in the whole sample. On the other hand, considerably
more caught offenders as well as selected juveniles have left school,
which also means low social status.

We analyzed a great number of family, school, work, and leisure variables for differences between the two offender groups, and
between the selected and nonselected juveniles. An interesting point
to note is that we found more significant differences between juveniles
selected on youth protection grounds and the other respondents than
between caught and noncaught offenders. Juveniles selected for judicial protection committed truancy more often, repeated more classes,
spent less time on homework, were punished more often, did not get
along so well with teachers, and disliked school much more. They
spent more of their leisure time outside the home and had more friends
with police contacts. No differences were found with respect to all
work variables, family variables, or friends. Selected juveniles are
essentially characterized by weaker school integration and more delinquent friends.

Detected offenders repeated classes more often and were more
often punished than the other offenders. They spent more time out-

side the home, went out more often with a large group, or alone, had
more delinquent friends, and more of them have had sexual relations.
Being caught by the police had seriously lessened their respect for
the police. However, the list of variables for which no differences
were found is much larger: all family variables, work variables,
variables about friends, truancy, running away, liking school, and
teachers. Detected offenders did not do so well at school, were
more emancipated from the family, and had more delinquent friends.
Still, they are more like the other offenders than different from them.
It appears, then, that discriminatory selection is greater with respect
to juveniles committing delinquent acts, than to juveniles selected on
youth protection grounds.

SUMMARY AND DISCUSSION

The main findings of this study can be summarized as follows·

1. Two-thirds of the interviewed juveniles reported some delinquent acts.
2. Most offenses are acts against property.
3. Most offenses are committed alone or in small groups.
4. Girls reported more offenses than expected; their delinquency was not much different from that of boys.
5. Except for aggressive delinquency, no relation with social
class could be established.
6. Children of foreigners reported less offenses than Belgian
children.
7. Pronounced delinquents are less attached to parents, teachers, or boss; relations with peers do not offer compensation for this
lack of attachment.
8. Pronounced delinquents have poor school records and greater
work instability.
9. Delinquent values appear to develop because of weaker relations with parents and teachers, and stronger relations with delinquent
friends.
10. Selection criteria for judicial intervention are frequency and
seriousness of delinquent behavior, sex, race, social class, and
broken family.
11. These criteria are more important in the case of the detection of offenders than in the case of selection of juveniles for judicial
protection.

Discussing these results, a few remarks are in order. In the
first place, the fact of committing some offenses during adolescence

seems to be perfectly normal. Differences between juveniles reporting no offenses and juveniles reporting one or two are small or nonexistent. Significant differences arose between offenders in the extreme delinquent categories and the others. So it is not the occasional
offender but the more pronounced one that should worry us. A second
remark concerns girls' delinquency. We may expect that in the future
girls' delinquency will be more like boys' delinquency. It is certainly
time that girls' delinquency received more attention from researchers.

   With respect to the theoretical implications of our findings, we
would like to stress that many of them have been previously established
by research on recorded delinquents. These results are thus mutually
supporting. But, in fact, many of the relations that persist in the case
of self-reported delinquency are generally weaker. As to selection
processes, our conclusion should be a prudent one: offenders as well
as juveniles selected on youth protection grounds scored high on variables shown to be related to pronounced delinquent behavior. But this
is not the whole story. The relation between pronounced delinquent
behavior and detection is far from perfect. In fact, detected juveniles
are not that much different from many nondetected ones. Judicial intervention is indeed a net with large holes through which many slip.
But who does slip through and who does not? The answer is that factors that have nothing to do with delinquent behavior also affect the
selection process.

REFERENCES

Anttila, I., and R. Jaakkola. 1966. "Unrecorded Criminality in Fin-
   land." Kriminologinen Tutkimuslaitos 2 (February): 17-26.

Article 36.2 of the Belgian Law on Youth Protection, August 4, 1965.

Bowlby, J. 1952. Maternal Care and Mental Health. The Hague:
   World Health Organization.

Buikhuisen, W., R. W. Jongman, and W. Oving. 1969. "Ongeregistreerde criminaliteit onder studenten." Nederlandische Tijdschrift voor criminologie 1 (June): 69-90.

Christie, N., J. Andenaes, and S. Skirbekk. 1965. "A Study in Self-
   Reported Crime." In Scandinavian Studies in Criminology, vol.
   1, edited by N. Christie, pp. 86-117. Oslo: Universitetsforlag.

Cicourel, A. V. 1968. "Police Practices and Official Records."
   The Social Organization of Juvenile Justice. New York: Wiley.

Cloward, R. A., and L. E. Ohlin. 1960. Delinquency and Opportunity. New York: Free Press.

Cohen, A. K. 1960. Delinquent Boys, the Culture of the Gang. New York: Free Press.

Elmhorn, K. 1965. "Study in Self-Reported Delinquency Among Schoolchildren in Stockholm." In Scandinavian Studies in Criminology, vol. 1, edited by N. Christie, pp. 117-47. Oslo: Universitetsforlag.

Ennis, P. H. 1973. "Crime, Victims and the Police." In Modern Criminals, edited by J. F. Short. New Brunswick, N.Y.: Dutton.

Erickson, M. L., and L. T. Empey. 1963. "Court Records, Undetected Delinquency and Decision-Making." Journal of Criminal Law, Criminal and Police Science 54 (December): 456-70.

Gold, H. 1970. Delinquent Behavior in an American City. Belmont, Calif.: Wadsworth.

Goldman, N. 1963. The Differential Selection of Juvenile Offenders for Court Appearance. Hackensack, N.J.: National Council on Crime and Delinquency.

Graven, J. 1965. "Le probleme des travailleurs etrangers delinquants en Suisse." Revue International de Criminologie et de Police Technologie 19 (November): 265-90.

Hirschi, T. 1972. Causes of Delinquency. Berkeley, Calif.: University of California Press.

Jongman, R. W. 1971. "Verborgen criminaliteit en sociale klasse." Nederlandische Tijdschrift voor Criminologie 1 (September): 141-54.

_____. 1972. "Ongeregistreerde criminaliteit onder vrouwelijke studenten." Nederlandische Tijdschrift voor Criminologie 1 (February): 1-12.

Jongman, R. W., and G. J. A. Smale. 1972. "De invloed van leeftijd, recidive en sociale klasse op het seponeringsbeleid." Nederlandische Tijdschrift voor Criminologie 1 (February): 30-36.

Junger-Tas, Josine. 1971. "La clientele de tribunal de la jeunesso. Etude statistique dans l'arrondissement de Bruxelles." Revue de Droit Penal et de Criminologie 1 (November): 163-93.

_____. 1973. "Integration sociale et delinquance juvenile." Revue de Droit Penal et de Criminologie 1 (February): 437-73.

Kaiser, G. 1971. Kriminologie, Eine Einführung in die Grundlagen. Karlsruhe: Verlag Müller.

Liben, G. 1963. "Un reflet de la criminalite italienne dans la region de Liege." Revue de Droit Penal et de Criminologie 44:265-90.

Matza, D. 1964. Delinquency and Drift. New York: Wiley.

McClintock, M. 1970. "Le chiffre noir." Etudes relatives a la recherche Criminologique 5 (Strasbourg).

Merton, R. K. 1957. Social Theory and Social Structure. New York: Free Press.

Miller, W. B. 1966. "Violent Crimes in City Gangs." The Annals of the American Academy of Political and Social Science 322 (March): 96-113.

_____. 1972. "Lower Class Culture as a Generating Milieu of Gang Delinquency." In Juvenile Delinquency: A Book of Readings, edited by R. Giallombardo, pp. 137-50. London: Wiley.

Murphy, F. J., M. M. Shirley, and H. L. Witmer. 1969. "The Incidence of Hidden Delinquency." In Deviance Studies in the Process of Stigmatization and Social Reaction, edited by S. Dinitz et al. London: Oxford University Press.

Myerhoff, J. L., and B. G. Myerhoff. 1967. "Field Observations of Middle Class Gangs." In Middle Class Juvenile Delinquency, edited by E. W. Vaz. New York: Harper & Row.

Nye, F. I. 1958. Family Relationships and Delinquent Behavior. New York: Macmillan.

Piliavin, I., and S. Briar. 1964. "Police Encounters with Juveniles." American Journal of Sociology 70 (September): 206-14.

Reckless, W. C. 1961. "A New Theory of Delinquency and Crime."
    Federal Probation 25 (December): 42–46.

Sellin, Thorsten. 1938. Culture Conflict and Crime. New York:
    Social Science Research Council.

Shannon, L. W. 1963. "Types and Patterns of Delinquency Referral
    in a Middle–Sized City." British Journal of Criminology 4 (July):
    24–37.

Short, J. F., and F. I. Nye. 1957. "Reported Behavior as a Criterion
    of Deviant Behavior." Social Problems 5 (Winter): 207–14.

Short, J. F., and F. L. Strodtbeck. 1965. Group Process and Gang
    Delinquency. Chicago: University of Chicago Press.

Sullivan, D. C., and L. J. Siegel. 1972. "How Police Use Informa-
    tion to Make Decisions." Crime and Delinquency 18 (July): 253–
    63.

Sykes, G., and D. Matza. 1957. "Techniques of Neutralization: A
    Theory of Delinquency." American Sociological Review 22 (De-
    cember): 664–70.

Terry, A. H. 1967. "Discrimination in the Handling of Juvenile
    Offenders by Social Control Agencies." Journal of Research in
    Crime and Delinquency 4 (July): 218–31.

VanBostraeten, H. 1974. La delinquance juvenile en Belgique en
    1969 et 1970. Brussels: Centre d'Etude de la Delinquence Ju-
    venile.

Vaz, E. W. 1966. "Selfreported Juvenile Delinquency and Socio-
    Economic Status." The Canadian Journal of Correction 8 (Jan-
    uary): 20–28.

Wolfgang, M. E., and F. Ferracuti. 1967. The Subculture of Vio-
    lence. London: Tavistock.

Yablonski, L. 1962. The Violent Gang. London: Pelican Books.

9

JUVENILE DELINQUENCY AND
NEW TOWNS: THE CASE OF ISRAEL
David Shichor
Alan Kirschenbaum

The focus of this chapter is to investigate the connections between socioeconomic factors and the extent and depth of juvenile delinquency in the social setting of Israeli development (new) towns.

Since World War II there have been rising rates of juvenile delinquency in most countries of the world. This phenomenon presents
a social problem and commands attention by policymakers, public officials, law enforcement agencies, youth workers, treatment organizations, social scientists, and large segments of the general public.

Israel, since its establishment in 1948, underwent a rapid process of industrialization and urbanization. At the same time, it also
experienced an unusually high rate of immigration. Official statistics
indicate that until the early 1970s there was a rising trend of delinquency in Israel, which leveled off in the last few years in volume;
but the rate of recidivism continued to increase, a trend that indicates
the formation and crystallization of a "hard core " delinquent group.
Amir and Hovav (1970) summed up some of the main characteristics
of juvenile delinquency in Israel:

1. The number of juvenile delinquents has gone up steadily
from 1948 to 1966. The proportion of Jewish juvenile delinquents
within their age groups increased from 6.7 per 1,000 to 21.2 per
1,000.

2. The number of juveniles charged has risen steadily; and
out of the total number of prosecutions, the share of the juveniles
has increased from 9.4 percent in 1950 to 33.1 percent in 1968.

3. Since 1948, there has been a steady increase in the average
number of recidivists. They accounted for 24.6 percent of the total
prosecutions in 1963, and for 31.1 percent in 1968.

At the same period of time, Israel, in trying to cope with the
large volume of immigration and its economic and security problems,
tried to establish development areas and new settlements. In these
areas several new towns were planned and built, and some existing
towns were replanned and settled mainly with newly arrived immigrants.
These are the so-called "development towns." The towns were planned
to answer three basic needs: to maximize security, to disperse the
population, and to serve as regional centers for agricultural areas.
Berler (1970) points out several shortcomings in regard to the establishment of these towns, especially in the processes of selection and
preparation of prospective settlers. They seem to be one of the main
factors adversely affecting the towns' socioeconomic development.

The formal criteria for defining urban settlements as "development towns" are the following: (1) They were established after 1948
or, if established earlier, received the greater part of their populations after this date; (2) the great majority of their populations consists of immigrants who came to Israel after 1948; and (3) they are
mainly located in the designated development areas of the country.
According to these criteria Berler (1970) classified 25 settlements
as "development towns," while Amiran and Shachar (1969), using a
somewhat less stringent definition, identified some 35 settlements as
fitting into this category.

Since this type of settlement was designated to fulfill important
functions in the absorption of immigrants and in the crystallization of
Israeli society, several works studying these towns, mainly from
ecological and demographic aspects, were published (Amiran and
Shachar, 1969; Berler, 1970; Comay and Kirschenbaum, 1973; Kirschenbaum, 1971; Kirschenbaum and Comay, 1973; Lichfield, 1971; and
Spiegel, 1967).

There are some other studies that investigated the social problems occurring in these towns. Among others, there are indications
that there is a serious problem of juvenile delinquency in these settlements. Amir and Max (1968) claim that the rates of juvenile delinquency in new, urban Israeli settlements and development towns are
unusually high, sometimes twice as high as the rate found in other
types of settlements. Shichor (1973), in an exploratory study of Israeli development towns dealing with this problem, found relationships between certain demographic indicators (internal migration,
population composition, and so on) and the rates of juvenile delinquency
in this type of social setting.

It is believed that the findings of the current study might provide
a valuable insight into the problem of juvenile delinquency in the unique
setting of new towns, which could be especially useful for those countries that might, for various reasons, be interested in establishing developing areas and new towns.

METHODOLOGY

A list of socioeconomic variables was drawn up, based on past research on juvenile delinquency (Berg, 1967; Fleischer, 1966; Schafer and Polk, 1967; Shoham, 1962; Voss and Peterson, 1971), social problems (Jahoda, Lazersfeld, and Zeisl, 1932; Fox-Piven and Cloward, 1972), and Israeli development towns (Cohen, 1970; Comay and Kirschenbaum, 1973; Kleff, 1973; Silverberg, 1972). This list of variables was subsequently reduced, due to restrictions and limitation of the available data. These variables cover a wide spectrum of socioeconomic factors that seem to have relevance to the phenomenon of juvenile delinquency, particularly in the context of development (new) towns. (See Table 9.1.)

The majority of the data were obtained from published documents of the Ministry of Housing and the Central Bureau of Statistics. Data on juvenile delinquency were compiled from several government sources, such as the Ministries of Welfare, Police, and Housing. Among the 25 urban areas designated as "development towns," only 16 were included in the study, due to lack of complete and comparable data. The problems of data were compounded by the variety of information sources with certain pieces of information available in one source but missing in another. The analysis was based only on 1968 material, which was the latest and most comprehensive available.

The dependent variable, juvenile delinquency, was analyzed in terms of rates per 1,000 population aged 10 to 19 in each town. The serious limitations of official data on crime and delinquency have been noted by many students in the field (Walker, 1971; Hood and Sparks, 1970; and so on), including the biases in the processes of defining, arresting, prosecuting, and convicting juvenile offenders (Piliavin and Briar, 1964; Werthman, 1967). Generally, it is a known fact that official rates of juvenile delinquency are underenumerated and tend to overemphasize the part of lower-class youths in juvenile delinquency. Since the current study was designed to be an exploratory one, it was decided to use the official data despite their limitations and to attempt the collection of more reliable data when an in-depth study of a larger scale will be undertaken.

To determine the strength and the relative importance of the socioeconomic components in explaining the variations in the delinquency rates of development towns, a stepwise multiple regression analysis was employed. The basic procedure of this analysis is to add additional variables into the regression with those accounting for the greatest proportion of variance appearing first, followed in order by those factors accounting for the greatest remaining variance. This procedure makes it possible to obtain the order of importance of each factor in explaining variations in the rates of juvenile delinquency.

TABLE 9.1

Summary of Factors and Operationalization

Generalized Concepts	Operationalization
General employment situation	Number unemployed or employed in public works per 1,000 in labor force
Quality of education	Students per class in kindergarten, and elementary school
Ethnic composition	Number native born per 1,000 population
Quality of housing	Density or number persons per room
Alternative available housing	Number of residential units completed per 1,000 in building stock
Level of health services	Number of full working days of general physicians per 1,000 population
Level of social/economic welfare	Number recipients receiving economic and noneconomic public support
Population stability	Number of in and out voluntary migrants per 1,000 population
Proximity to large urban center	Distance to nearest large ubran place (kilometers)
Older versus newer towns	Year of founding
Social/political integration	Proportion of population voting in national and local elections

Source: Compiled by the authors.

The initial runs were attempted to weed out highly intercorrelated variables, which would confound the analysis. Additionally, as the regression proceeded, the computer program automatically ascertained the relative weights of the variables in relation to their tolerance levels and F scores for each variable at each step of the analysis. As an added precaution, the few variables highly correlated were dropped from further analysis.

The results of the analysis reveal that an unusually high percent of variance—84.2 percent—is explained (see Table 9.2). It is important to point out that, although the total variance explained is high, given the small number of towns and the fairly large number of varia-

TABLE 9.2

Relationships Between Socioeconomic Variables and the Extent of
Juvenile Delinquency

Component	Change in R^2*		Level of Significance
Unemployment	22.5		< .01
Overcrowding in elementary schools	22.4	66.3	< .01
Year of founding	10.7	percent	< .01
Proportion of native born	10.7		< .01
Welfare recipients	8.1		n.s.
Number of general physicians	2.9		n.s.
Construction rates	2.9	17.9	n.s.
Overcrowding in high schools	1.7	percent	n.s.
Distance from urban center	1.0		n.s.
Density per house unit	1.3		n.s.
Total variance explained		84.2 percent	

*All the relationships between the socioeconomic variables and
juvenile delinquency are positive.

Note: n.s. = not significant.

Source: Compiled by the authors.

bles examined, this was to be expected. Four variables—the extent
of unemployment, the quality of elementary education, year of founding, and the proportion of natives born in the town—accounted for
66.3 percent of the variance. A deeper examination of the relationships between these variables and juvenile delinquency in the social
setting of Israeli development towns is in order.

DISCUSSION

Unemployment in an achievement-oriented, modern industrial
society is "both an economic and a personal problem" (Rose, 1967, p.
584). Economically, it hurts the family and often it causes poverty
and all the problems that poverty entails. Additionally, it has sociopsychological repercussions on the individual and disruptive impacts

on traditional modes of behavior in the family and community (Jahoda, Lazarsfeld, and Zeisl, 1932). It might seriously affect one's self-concept and cause personal insecurity.

> When a father, who was the sole breadwinner of a family is no longer able to support his family because he can not find work, either the family will become dependent on outside sources, or the mother and/or the older children will become the earners. Obviously, this change affects the father's image and status in the family. . . . If the family is not flexible enough to readjust quickly to this changed role relationship—the family is likely to disintegrate. (Rose, 1967, p. 584)

This disintegration means also that the family is no longer able to exercise effective control over the behavior of the children, and this function passes to a large extent to the youths' peer group.

This is a familiar process in Israel, where a large percentage among those adult males who immigrated from Moslem countries did not possess the occupational skills required in a modern industrial economy and became unemployed, underemployed, or employed in jobs considered to have very low prestige (Shichor, 1974). It is probably more so in the development towns, since, in the great majority of them, there is a high concentration of immigrants from Moslem countries with a very low level of formal educational attainment (Shichor, 1973).

The quality of education also had a high explanatory value of juvenile delinquency in these towns. In modern, urbanized industrial societies, educational achievement is one of the main indicators of social status and a major avenue toward social mobility. There are indications that the general quality of education in Israeli development towns is lower than in other urban centers. (At the beginning of the 1974–75 school year in one town, the parents closed down the elementary school, protesting its low standards; and the Ministry of Education had to promise that it would make sincere efforts to raise the scholastic standards by changing some of the teachers.) One of the indicators of this phenomenon is the relatively low percentage of youth in the 14- to 17-year age group who attend high school (which is not compulsory in Israel) in these towns; and the extremely low percentage of university students (Berler, 1970, pp. 159, 161). An even more serious problem is the difficulty in attracting highly qualified teachers to development towns, mainly due to reasons of social and cultural isolation. Thus, large percentages of the teachers are not permanent residents of these towns, and many of them do not yet have their permanent teacher's certificate (Berler, 1970, p. 60). The turnover among teachers is unusually high.

As an indicator of the quality of elementary education, the indirect measure of overcrowding—pupil-to-class ratio—was examined. Teaching conditions are influenced by the number of children present in the classroom and the amount of attention that the teacher must divide among them. It obviously also affects the social control functions of the school and its attractiveness in the eyes of many youngsters. It very likely is connected with overt or covert dropout rates as well. This links it to the problems of juvenile delinquency.

Another factor with a significant explanatory value of variance was the year the town was founded. All but one of the 16 towns were established after 1948 (the year of independence), and the great majority of their populations consist of immigrants who came to Israel after that date. The towns were divided into two groups: (1) seven towns that were founded between 1948 and 1953 at the time of the great wave of immigration (one of them was established before but received more than 75 percent of its inhabitants after 1948); and (2) nine towns that were established after 1953. It was found that in the newer towns, the rates of juvenile delinquency were significantly higher (on the .01 level of significance) than in the towns established before 1953. There are some factors that might be related to these findings. At least two of them are worthy of mention. First, in the newer towns the proportion of youngsters is higher in the general population. As Shichor (1973, p. 98) points out, this phenomenon makes family control and informal social controls applicable to a lesser degree in these towns. It also increases the opportunity for "differential association" among the youngsters, and especially among those who are prone to commit delinquent acts. Second, these towns were established in the wake of an influx of a large-scale immigration from underdeveloped countries, and the towns recruited the majority of their settlers from this group. This population is socially more "problematic," and a large proportion of it experienced severe social disorganization after the immigrants' arrival to Israel. These findings tend to contradict, partially, the high rates of delinquency among youngsters of Kirschenbaum's and Comay's assumption that "newer towns benefited from mistakes made in earlier towns" (1973, p. 689).

The proportion of Israelis born in each town explained 10.7 percent of the total variance and was statistically significant on the .01 level. According to the findings, the higher the proportion of native-born members of the population, the higher are the rates of juvenile delinquency in the development towns. Since the native-born category includes almost exclusively the younger age groups in these settlements (the children of the immigrant settlers), the problems of social control, as it was already pointed out, are more severe when the proportion of this group is higher in the population of the town.

Although in the current study the ethnic origin of the parents of the native born was not investigated, Shichor (1973) found that the overwhelming majority came from Asian–African countries. This is in line with Amir's and Shichor's (1975) study of the ethnic aspects of juvenile delinquency in Israel. It seems that the "culture conflict" proposition of Sellin (1938), which suggests that second–generation immigrant youngsters are the most prone to get involved in delinquency since they are the most exposed to experience the opposing impacts of the value system of immigrant groups on the one hand and the norms prevailing in the receiving society on the other hand, holds true for Israel. The validity of this proposition to the Israeli scene in the 1950s was already demonstrated by Shoham (1962). The broader the cultural and economic disparity between a given ethnic group and the normative system (presumably East European), the higher is the juvenile delinquency rate. This might explain, at least partially, the high rates of delinquency among youngsters of Asian–African origin (Shoham, Shoham and Abd–El–Razek, 1966; Amir–Hovav, 1970; Shichor–Arad, 1974; Amir and Shichor, 1975).

These four variables—the extent of unemployment, the quality of elementary education, the year of founding, and the proportion of native born in the settlement—have been statistically significant in explaining the phenomenon of juvenile delinquency in Israeli development towns (see Table 9.3). They explained 66.3 percent of the variance. The other six variables accounted for 17.9 percent of the variance, and they were not statistically highly significant; however, all of them indicated a positive relationship with juvenile delinquency (see Table 9.2). Among these six variables, the "proportion of welfare recipients" explained the highest proportion, 8.1 percent, of the variance. This finding is also in the expected direction, since the dependence on welfare, aside from indicating the economic situation, also has ramifications for the extent of social disorganization. Inter-

TABLE 9.3

Age Distribution in New Towns

Age	New Towns	Older Towns	Total Jewish Population
0–14	40.5	31.6	34.8
15–64	55.2	61.5	59.9
65+	4.3	6.9	5.3
Total	100.0	100.0	100.0

Source: Alexander Berler, New Towns in Israel (Jerusalem: Hebrew University Press, 1970), p. 68.

estingly, although this variable had a "primary significance in determining the attractiveness of the towns" (Kirschenbaum and Comay,
1973, p. 691), it was not highly significant (statistically) to juvenile
delinquency.

RECIDIVISM

Recidivism is still the most widely accepted indicator of the extent of "success" or "failure" of the preventive efforts and intervention activities of the various agencies of social control in the field of
juvenile delinquency. Usually in Israel, a large part of the first offenders do not return to officially known delinquent behavior. A recent five-years' follow-up study of young juvenile delinquents showed
only a 23.4 percent official recidivism rate (Shichor-Arad, 1974).
Although research on undetected delinquency indicates that most adolescent boys are sporadically involved in some kind of behavior that
constitutes offense (Erickson and Empey, 1963), those who are "repeatedly convicted are usually the worst offenders" (West, 1967, p.
41). Similarly, Gibbons (1970) points out that delinquent behavior
is rather a matter of quantity than quality, the most repetitious offenders being the "hard-core" delinquents.
In this study an attempt was made to investigate the socioeconomic
variables that might contribute to the evolvement of a "hard-core"
group of delinquents in the context of Israeli development towns.
Again, a stepwise, multiple regression analysis was employed to reveal the patterns of relationships between the rates of recidivism and
the formerly analyzed socioeconomic variables.
The results in Table 9.4 indicate that, again, there is an unusually high percentage of explained variance—82.2 percent. As in the
case of general juvenile delinquency, the rate of unemployment and
the overcrowding of elementary schools (which was used as an indicator of the "quality of schooling") seem to have the most effective
explanatory capability of juvenile recidivism in these towns. These
two factors accounted for 44.6 percent of the variance and were statistically significant on the .05 level. They showed a positive relationship with recidivism. Two other variables that showed a statistically
significant relationship with the rate of recidivism were density per
dwelling unit and distance from larger population centers. These
two variables together explained 18.7 percent of the total variance.
The relationship between density (the average number of persons per dwelling unit) and juvenile recidivism was positive; that is,
in new towns where density is higher, there are significantly higher
rates of recidivism among youthful offenders. It is interesting to
point out that the very same variable of density per dwelling unit was

only a poor indicator of the rates of juvenile delinquency. This factor seems to have an explanatory value only in the case of the more severe delinquents.

The distance from larger population centers was negatively related to juvenile recidivism; that is, the farther away a new town was located from big cities, the lower were the rates of recidivism among juveniles. A theoretically plausible explanation for this finding is that the farther away and more isolated the community is from large population centers, the more cohesive (Gemeinschaft type) social nature it will have; and the means of informal social control will be stronger and more frequently used. This finding seems to be somewhat in accordance with one of Shoham et al.'s (1970) hypotheses; namely, that the highest rates of juvenile delinquency and its most serious forms will occur in the more urbanized and culturally more complex settlements.

Three other variables—the proportion of the native (Israeli-born) juvenile delinquents whose parents were also born in Israel, the proportion of the native (Isreali-born) settlers, and the proportion of the juvenile delinquents of European-American origin (either they themselves or their parents)—together contributed 18.9 percent to the explanation of the total variance, although they were not significant on the .05 level of statistical significance.

TABLE 9.4

Relationships Between Socioeconomic Variables and Recidivism

Component	Change in R^2		Level of Significance
Unemployment	+ 22.4		< .05
Overcrowding in elementary schools	+ 22.2	63.3	< .05
Density	+ 9.8	percent	< .05
Distance	− 8.9		< .05
Proportion of native juvenile delinquents	− 8.0	18.9	n.s.
Proportion of native settlers	+ 5.8	percent	n.s.
Proportion of European/ American juvenile delinquents	+ 5.1		n.s.
Total variance explained		82.2 percent	

Note: n.s. = not significant.

Source: Compiled by the authors.

CONCLUSION

The basic aim of this brief study has been to explore the extent and depth of juvenile delinquency in Israeli development (new) towns, and to investigate the connections between this phenomenon and a set of socioeconomic indicators. This study, as does Kirschenbaum and Shichor's study (1975), indicates some statistically significant relationships between the extent of unemployment, the quality of elementary schooling, the date of founding of the town, the proportion of Israeli-borns in the development town, and the rates of juvenile delinquency. Furthermore, there were some additional relationships that did not reach statistical significance but still might have explanatory value for the understanding of the delinquency problem in this social setting.

Similarly, there were significant relationships between unemployment, the quality of elementary schooling, density per dwelling unit, distance from larger population centers, and the extent of juvenile recidivism.

In this chapter an attempt was made to find some explanation for these relationships on the basis of the existing knowledge in this field of study. The two outstanding socioeconomic factors that seem to be highly connected both with the extent of juvenile delinquency and with the rate of recidivism were the rate of unemployment and the quality of elementary education. These are not newly discovered factors in delinquency research, but it is important to confirm that they also carry an important weight in the social setting of new development towns.

This small-scale study sheds some light on the social problems occurring in this new type of settlement, which was planned to solve some of the problems of a new immigrant society. It is hoped that these findings will encourage additional research in this area and will help the government agencies to implement changes in existing programs or to start new ones that will cope with the problems of social disorganization in this type of social setting. Some of the findings might be useful also for other countries contemplating the establishment of new towns for various reasons.

REFERENCES

Amir, Menachem, and Meir Hovav. 1970. "Juvenile Delinquency in Isreal." In Children and Families in Israel, edited by A. Jarus, J. Marcus, J. Oren, and C. Rapaport. New York: Gordon and Beach.

Amir, Menachem, and David Max. 1968. Child Delinquency (in Hebrew). Jerusalem: Henrietta Szold Institute.

Amir, Menachem, and David Shichor. 1975. "Ethnic Aspects of Juvenile Delinquency in Israel" (in Hebrew). Crime and Social
Deviance 3 (Spring): 1-19; 3 (Summer): 1-15.

Amiram, D. H. K., and Shachar. 1969. Development Towns in Israel. Jerusalem: Hebrew University Press.

Berg, Ivan. 1967. "Economic Factors in Delinquency." In Task
Force Report—Juvenile Delinquency and Youth Crime. Washington, D.C.: U.S. Government Printing Office.

Berler, Alexander. 1970. New Towns in Israel. Jerusalem: Hebrew University Press.

Cohen, Erik. 1970. "Development Towns—The Social Dynamics of
'Planted' Urban Communities." In Integration and Development
in Israel, edited by S. N. Eisenstadt. Jerusalem: Hebrew University Press.

Comay, Yochanan, and Alan Kirschenbaum. 1973. "The Israeli New
Town: An Experiment at Population Redistribution." Economic
Development and Cultural Change 22 (October): 124-B4.

Erickson, Maynard L., and Lamar T. Empey. 1963. "Court Records, Undetected Delinquency and Decision Making." The Journal of Criminal Law, Criminology and Police Science 54 (December): 456-69.

Fleisher, Belton M. 1966. The Economics of Delinquency. Chicago:
Quadrangle.

Gibbons, Don C. 1970. Delinquent Behavior. Englewood Cliffs,
N.J.: Prentice-Hall.

Hood, Roger, and Richard Sparks. 1970. Key Issues in Criminology.
London: World University Library.

Jahoda, Marie, Paul F. Lazarsfeld, and Hans Zeisl. 1932. Die Ar-
beitslosen von Marienthal. Leipzig, Germany: Staatsforlag.

Kirschenbaum, Alan. 1971. "Selective Migration and Population Redistribution: A Study of New Towns in Israel." Center for Urban and Regional Studies 2. Haifa: Technion.

Kirschenbaum, Alan, and Yochanan Comay. 1973. "Dynamics of Population Attraction to New Towns in Israel." Socio-Economic Planning Sciences 7 (December): 687-96.

Kirschenbaum, Alan, and David Shichor. 1975. "Population Dispersion as a Social Experiment: New Towns and Delinquency in Israel." Unpublished manuscript.

Kleff, Vivian Z. 1973. "Ethnic Segregation in Urban Israel." Demography 10 (May): 161-84.

Lichfield, Nathaniel. 1971. Israel's New Towns: A Development Strategy. Jerusalem: Israel Ministry of Housing.

Piliavin, Irving, and Scott Briar. 1964. "Police Encounters with Criminals." American Journal of Sociology 70 (September): 206-14.

Piven, Frances Fox, and Richard A. Cloward. 1972. Regulating the Poor. London: Tavistock.

Rose, Arnold M. 1967. Sociology: The Study of Human Relations. New York: Knopf.

Schafer, Walter E., and Kenneth Polk. 1967. "Delinquency and the Schools." In Task Force Report: Juvenile Delinquency and Youth Crime. Washington, D.C.: U.S. Government Printing Office.

Sellin, Thorsten. 1938. Culture Conflict and Crime. New York: Social Science Research Council.

Shichor, David. 1973. "Some Correlates of Juvenile Delinquency in Israel Development Towns." In Israel Studies in Criminology, vol. 2, edited by S. Shoham. Jerusalem: Jerusalem Academic Press.

_____. 1974. "Perceived 'School Experience' of 'Continuing' and 'Non-Continuing' Delinquents in Israel." Paper delivered at the Eighth World Congress of Sociology, Toronto, August.

Shichor, David, and Shlomo Arad. 1974. Follow-up of Young Delinquents in Israel. Jerusalem: Henrietta Szold Institute.

Shoham, Shlomo. 1962. "The Application of the 'Culture Conflict' Hypothesis to the Criminality of Immigrants in Israel." Journal of Criminal Law, Criminology, and Police Science 53 (June): 79–87.

Shoham, Shlomo, Nahum Shoham, and Adnan Abd–El–Razek. 1970. "Immigration, Ethnicity and Ecology as Related to Juvenile Delinquency in Israel." In Israel Studies in Criminology, vol. 1, edited by S. Shoham. Jerusalem: Jerusalem Academic Press.

Silverberg, Ruth. 1972. "Distribution of Israel's Population: 1948–1972" (in Hebrew). Ministry of the Treasury, General Planning Authority, Research Publication Series No. 4. Jerusalem (Hebrew).

Spiegel, E. 1967. New Towns in Israel: Urban and Regional Planning Development. New York: Praeger.

Voss, Harwin L., and David M. Petersen, eds. 1971. Ecology, Crime, and Delinquency. New York: Appleton–Century, Crofts.

Walker, Nigel. 1971. Crimes, Courts and Figures: An Introduction to Criminal Statistics. London: Penguin.

Werthman, Carl. 1967. "The Function of Social Definitions in the Development of Delinquent Careers." In Task Force Report: Juvenile Delinquency and Youth Crime. Washington, D.C.: U.S. Government Printing Office.

West, D. J. 1967. The Young Offender. London: Penguin.

10

DELINQUENCY PREVENTION
THROUGH FATHER TRAINING:
SOME OBSERVATIONS
AND PROPOSALS
Leo Davids

Given the magnitude of today's crime and delinquency problem
in most modern societies and the undeniable failure of the correctional
strategies currently used, the search for ways to prevent delinquency
has become absolutely vital. There is considerable research now on
its causes and control, with a view to breaking the vicious cycles that
escalate young people toward delinquency before the youth is caught in
the criminal justice system's rounds of probation, failure, incarceration, and a long-term career of recidivism.

Even prior to the classic Unraveling Juvenile Delinquency (Glueck
and Glueck, 1950), some researchers focused on the family as the most
logical point of departure for an analysis of how delinquency starts.
There is some consensus in the literature that many criminal careers
begin with disturbances of socialization during childhood.

More specifically, parental failure as agents of socialization
combined with criminogenic environmental factors such as the pro-
criminal peer group, failure and frustration at school, and such have
been viewed as antical in the development of youth crime and delinquency (Reiss, 1971; Jeffery and Jeffery, 1967; Hirschi, 1971, chap.
6). Investigators have repeatedly pointed to problems of inconsistent
discipline, lack of communication and emotional warmth between
parents and children, as well as low identification with the adult male
role as important variables in the etiology of major behavior disturbances during adolescence and later life (Andry, 1971; Pringle, 1975;
Sebald, 1976; Tec, 1970). It has also been shown that satisfactory
relationships with adults correlate with lower peer group involvement,
with apparent increases to compensate for poor interaction with significant adults (Iacovetta, 1975). These sociopsychological difficulties
tend to occur in clusters rather than singly and generally are associated with patterns of poor parenting, which give the child a poorer

chance than other children in his community to grow up in the conventional way and stay out of trouble (Menzies, 1965, chap. 2; Rubenfeld, 1965).

This chapter assumes that for the older child and older adolescent the father's role may, in many cases, be more significant than that of the mother. It is therefore reasonable to assume that more effective parenting—especially by fathers—should produce better socialization, higher identification with conventional roles and conventional values, and therefore lead to a smaller proportion of serious or long-term delinquents (Hindelang, 1973). Prevention of delinquency, then, is to be accomplished by improving the psychocultural and sociological environment in the homes of delinquents or those who run a high categoric risk of becoming involved with delinquency. This requires some actual changes of behavior by parents (Benson, 1968, pp. 262–63; Jeffery and Jeffery, 1967, pp. 92–96).

It should be noted here that we are not talking about broken homes per se—that is, father absence. The important issues are not necessarily tied to the presence of the male parent in the home, but refer to what the male contributes to the child's development. That is, a substitute for the father could be just as effective as the biological father if his contribution to the child's socialization is good. On the other hand, uninterrupted presence of the father may be of little consequence or may even contribute to delinquency if his influence turns out to be pernicious in terms of subsequent antisocial behavior (Benson, 1968, pp. 263–64; Grygier et al., 1969). Pathological noninvolvement and weakness by fathers has been indicated by various authors tracing the etiology of mental and behavioral disorders (Rubenfeld, 1965, pp. 174–79, 291–94; Sebald, 1976, pp. 210–14), but the evidence is understandably hard to obtain and rests frequently in clinical observations and hypotheses rather than on direct monitoring of paternal behavior.

It has frequently been pointed out that the father's role today is challenging and difficult, but in Western civilization men receive neither training nor sufficient relevant models to imitate in preparation for functioning as a father. In postindustrial society, the problems of fatherhood are considerably more troublesome than those in agrarian and industrializing societies, despite the fact that schools and material conditions have improved (LeMasters, 1974, chaps. 1, 4, and 8; Davids, 1972).

Among the consequences of this failure by the society to support the entry of men into the father role and to provide suitable training for functioning in this area is the steady rise in juvenile delinquency over the past few decades. Although most of the economic, educational, and other widely discussed factors that were formerly blamed for delinquency have been dealt with to some extent, the problems of

ill-equipped parents (again, our emphasis being on the father) have
not been touched at all.

Some have proposed the substitution of more acceptable parenting by removing the child to a foster home as a good solution to this
kind of problem (Menzies, 1964, pp. 95-99; Grygier et al., 1969, p.
250). What we are looking at, however, is the possibility of improving parental performance in the boy's own home, at much less risk to
the child and less cost to society. The strategy of foster care appears
not to be succeeding, and it would be far more practical to give intervention at home a chance to demonstrate its worth.

Andry's (1971) classic study and other evidence in the literature
(Robins, 1975; Tec, 1970) reinforces our argument that the role of
the father in delinquency causation is significant. It follows that it
would be a wise strategy to attempt the prevention of delinquency
through the fathers of children already identified as predelinquent behavior problems, or as delinquent. This requires systematic attention if we are to make any real dent in the production of delinquency
within the family. The juvenile courts would accept as major tasks
the identification of cases where father training is called for, and see-
ing to it that these men would enroll in and attend the classes. Where
the authority of the court has to be used, it should be applied in a sensitive way to produce consistent father participation in the program
with the least resentment possible.

The objective of such a program is to guide the parents of troubled and consistently misbehaving children to increase their self-confidence and to improve their performance as models, coaches, and
disciplinarians. There are a number of areas in which the capacities
and performance of fathers should be improved: for example, the
linkage between the family and the school, between the family and the
juvenile justice system, and the direct relationship between father
and child.

It should be observed that the kind of intervention strategy that
is being discussed in this chapter has, in fact, been tried. The summary by Novick on "Community Programs and Projects" (1960) lists
this kind of education as a project that had actually been tried in the
1950s (see also Tefferteller, 1959). It is worth quoting from Novick

> Special parent groups are set up in local agencies, such
> as neighbourhood houses, where they discuss a wide range
> of subjects related to child rearing, family life, and com-
> munity problems that contribute to delinquency. The sup-
> port that the parents get from each other and from knowing
> that others are struggling with similar problems seem to be
> one of the most important aspects of these programs. (No-
> vick, 1960, pp. 8-9)

Perhaps the ideas about parent training that have been raised (Crow, 1968; Davids, 1971; Hawkins, 1971; McIntire, 1974; Sebald, 1975, p. 250) do betray a middle-class bias in that a parent education program may be less likely to succeed with lower-class fathers than with middle-class ones. Middle-class fathers, who have had secondary and higher education, would more likely relate better to an organized teaching setup. The social class differences in this regard have been discussed by Jeffery and Jeffery (1967, pp. 94-96) and Johnson and Katz (1973, p. 186). Nevertheless, it is reasonable to expect that delinquency prevention through programs of education for parents whose children have begun to show active difficulties would have more success than delinquency control programs that come on the scene entirely post facto, too late to do any good.

The question we must now briefly consider is how the prevention of delinquency along the lines that we have been discussing might be accomplished. In other words, what tactics for intervention in family dynamics—before the delinquency problem has developed fully and "hardened"—should we recommend? Following the literature on parent training for dealing with mental retardation and other handicaps (Clement, 1971; Stott, 1972; Tymchuk, 1973), as well as the several authors who have actually touched on parent training specifically for controlling antisocial and delinquent behavior, a few general suggestions are in order.

As Tefferteller (1959), Crow (1968), and Wiltz (1969) suggest, the preferred mode of accomplishing the desired changes in parent behavior seems to be intensive work with small groups of parents. As shown in the comprehensive review by Johnson and Katz (1973), it is clear that many serious attempts have been made to bring together parents who face similar problems (which in itself reassures them and starts providing the basis of self-confidence that they would require to make any effective changes in their own homes) and to proceed with relatively short-term programs of instruction based essentially on behavior modification techniques. From a cost-benefit standpoint, small-group strategies are efficient for this kind of education. Thus, we already find in the literature reports from projects that try to explain something about learning and reinforcement theory to parents, after which practical implementation of the theory in specific techniques has been attempted, both in laboratory classroom settings and at home (see Brown, 1976, and the popular parent-training movement today). Tymchuk (1973) and Becker (1971, p. 1) have worked extensively in this area, and they point out that there have been some successes in programs of this kind.

It should certainly be possible to apply to the parents of many delinquents, especially the fathers, those procedures for improving parenting behavior that have been discussed by such authors as Becker

(1971), Hawkins (1971), McIntire (1974), and Stott (1972). These programs of parent training, again, are based on changing overt behavior rather than personality dynamics or underlying emotional states, and they have demonstrated that a quite limited input of professional time can bring about favorable results. Cost factors are terribly important in reality, if not in laboratory situations, and so this method has been strongly advocated on resources/efficiency grounds (Clement, 1971, p. 65; Johnson and Katz, 1973, pp. 181, 196). These same elements would be crucial in father training for delinquency prevention.

Perhaps it is possible to summarize the root of the fathers and delinquency problem as, to a large extent, crucial ignorance. There are also psychological limitations in the fathers; but, to some extent, these may well be aggravated by major cognitive lacunae (Sebald, 1976, pp. 246–49). If ignorance is the basis of the unsatisfactory performance by many fathers (rather than ill will or nonmotivation of any sort), an educational approach should provide the solution. The ignorance that we are concerned about is roughly divisible into two areas.

1. The significant environment of today's urban adolescent, including the modern high school, television, and the peer group. One has to know something about their nature, and how each makes its impact on the adolescent, his identity, and his attitudes.

2. How the parent–child process works during late childhood and adolescence (not in early childhood), including techniques that can increase the closeness and openness of communication between father and youth; identification with parents and role modeling; and how to encourage consistently healthy and worthwhile directions of growth.

The substantive content of an antidelinquency program, therefore, would have to fill (or try to) these gaps so the men emerge at least acquainted with the framework of their children's world, and with the beginnings of a constructive and supportive stance toward youth. These are the general goals of such an instructional effort aimed at this specific type of learner, on the cognitive plane; there are also psychoemotional facets that we touch on later. But these are latent functions of the group experience, rather than part of the "syllabus" or curriculum.

Since one can find some descriptions, in the literature cited herein, of the topics, mechanics, and procedures that are usually involved in parent training, it is sufficient here to note some specific points about the substance of the educational program envisioned in this chapter.

FACULTY

The necessary teachers for the fathers of delinquents could be recruited initially from among social workers who have been involved with treating family conflict, as well as some law enforcement personnel who have specialized in youth work, probation counseling of juveniles, and so on. In time, a corps of experienced father-educators would be generated by the ongoing activities, and the personnel problem solves itself in the normal manner.

OBJECTIVES

The fathers would have to be given some basic understanding of child and adolescent psychology, focusing on motivation; the effects of peer groups and other social factors; as well as the development and change of personal identity. Such cognitive instruction would have to be accompanied and followed by genuinely relevant and audience-sensitive workshop sessions in the handling of difficult behavior, effective discussion of important long-term problems with teachers and other personnel outside the home, and approaches to understanding the behavior of children as not merely reflections of their inner dispositions and choices, but as messages to the parents about the child's state of mind, his worries, and problems.

METHODS

Through educational tactics such as role playing, the use of video tape for self-awareness and (group) self-criticism, and the sharing of successful and unsuccessful experiences in group discussion among people who are basically "in the same boat," it is likely that considerable changes can be brought about even when dealing with a population whose educational level is not high or with those who have not had such experience with, or exposure to, any aspect of the behavioral sciences.

Although some fathers may emerge unimproved from a program that attempts to change their outlook on child rearing, it is likely, as previous research suggests, that there would be real improvement in a large number of homes. Given the great cost-efficiency benefits of using parents in the control of antisocial and delinquent behavior, and the continuing low success rates with present methods of delinquency control, we can hardly lose by continuing with action research along these lines on a large scale.

SUMMARY

To review the argument herein, we may emphasize the following propositions:

1. Fathers have an important part to play in the socialization
of children and adolescents, and it is not merely presence or absence
that counts. Bad socialization can occur through "sins" of omission
or commission.

2. It is possible to change role performance of parents (including fathers) significantly by suitable programs of adult education that
are geared to the intended audience and use modern teaching techniques, which have proven effective where conventional reading and
lecturing would not work.

3. Juvenile courts should aim at early identification of juvenile
delinquency with a significant family etiology and use their power in a
sophisticated way to enroll many of the fathers in such an educational
program as early as possible. The sooner that these parents change
their ways in regard to such areas as discipline and guidance, the
less likely is further trouble by these children.

4. The potential savings in regard to effectiveness in controlling juvenile delinquency as opposed to the present methods of using
expensive therapy and other case-by-case professional intervention,
or full-time institutional placement, make it extremely likely that the
strategy presented in this chapter will give good results and will demonstrate that there is something we can do about preventing and controlling juvenile delinquency.

Specifically, it is here proposed that the juvenile courts should
consider not only the appropriate disposition for the young people
that come before them but also should impose such an education requirement on certain of their parents, where relevant shortcomings
of the latter are exposed. This writer can think of no more direct
approach than what has been discussed here.

REFERENCES

Andry, Robert G. 1971. Delinquency and Parental Pathology. London: Staples Press.

Becker, Wesley. 1971. Parents Are Teachers. Champaign, Ill.:
Research Press.

Benson, Leonard. 1968. Fatherhood: A Sociological Perspective.
New York: Random House.

Biller, H. B., and D. L. Meredith. 1972. "The Invisible American
    Father." Sexual Behaviour 2 (July): 16–22.

Brown, Catherine C. 1976. "It Changed My Life." Psychology To-
    day, November, pp. 47–57.

Clement, Paul W. 1971. "Please, Mother, I'd Rather You Did It
    Yourself: Training Parents to Treat Their Own Children."
    Journal of School Health 41 (February): 65–69.

Crow, Maxine S. 1968. "A Promising Method for Problem Preven-
    tion—Parent Education in Small Groups." Juvenile Court Judges'
    Journal 19 (September): 104–07.

Davids, Leo. 1971. "North American Marriage: 1990." The Fu-
    turistic 5 (October): 190–94.

_____. 1972. "Fatherhood and Comparative Social Research." In-
    ternational Journal of Comparative Sociology 13 (September):
    217–22.

Glueck, S., and E. Glueck. 1950. Unraveling Juvenile Delinquency.
    New York: Commonwealth Fund.

Grygier, T., J. Chesley, and Elizabeth W. Tuters. 1969. "Parental
    Deprivation: A Study of Delinquent Children." British Journal
    of Criminology 9 (July): 209–53.

Hawkins, Robert P. 1971. "Universal Parenthood Training." Edu-
    cation Technology 11 (February): 28–31.

Hindelang, Michael J. 1973. "Causes of Delinquency: A Partial
    Replication and Extension." Social Problems 20 (Spring): 471–87.

Hirschi, Travis. 1971. The Causes of Delinquency. Berkeley: Uni-
    versity of California Press.

Iacovetta, R. G. 1975. "Adolescent-Adult Interaction and Peer
    Group Involvement." Adolescence 10 (Fall): 327–36.

Jeffery, C. R., and I. A. Jeffery. 1967. "Prevention Through the
    Family." In Delinquency Prevention, edited by W. E. Amos
    and C. F. Wellford. Englewood Cliffs, N.J.: Prentice-Hall.

Johnson, Claudia A., and Roger C. Katz. 1973. "Using Parents as Change Agents for Their Children: A Review." Journal of Child Psychology and Psychiatry 14 (September): 181–200.

LeMasters, E. E. 1974. Parents in Modern America. Homewood, Ill.: Dorsey.

McIntire, Roger W. 1974. "Parenthood Training or Mandatory Birth Control: Take Your Choice." In The Future of Sexual Relations, edited by R. T. Francoeur and A. K. Francoeur, pp. 94–102. Englewood Cliffs, N.J.: Prentice-Hall (Spectrum S-350).

Menzies, D. W. 1965. The Grey People. Melbourne: Cassell Australia.

Novick, Mary B. 1960. Community Programs and Projects for the Prevention of Delinquency. Washington, D.C.: Department of Health, Education and Welfare, Children's Bureau.

Pringle, Mia Kellmer. 1975. The Needs of Children. New York: Schocken.

Reiss, Ira L. 1971. The Family System in America. New York: Holt, Rinehart and Winston, chap. 22.

Robins, Lee N., P. A. West, and B. L. Herjanic. 1975. "Arrests and Delinquency in Two Generations: A Study of Black Urban Families and Their Children." Journal of Child Psychology and Psychiatry 16 (April): 125–40.

Rubenfeld, Seymour. 1975. Family of Outcasts. New York: Free Press.

Sebald, Hans. 1976. Momism (The Silent Disease of America). Chicago: Nelson Hall.

Stott, D. H. 1972. The Parent as Teacher. Toronto: New Press.

Tec, Nechama. 1970. "Family and Differential Involvement with Marijuana: A Study of Suburban Teenagers." Journal of Marriage and the Family 32 (November): 656–64.

Tefferteller, Ruth S. 1959. "Delinquency Prevention Through Revitalizing Parent–Child Relations." The Annals 322 (March): 69–78.

Tymchuk, Alexander J. 1973. "Parents as Trainers of Mentally Re-
    tarded and Emotionally Disturbed Children." Paper presented
    at Canadian Psychological Association meeting, Victoria, B.C.,
    June 7–9.

Wiltz, Nicholas A. 1969. "Modification of Behaviors of Deviant Boys
    Through Parent Participation in a Group Technique." Ph.D.
    thesis, University of Oregon.

Winslow, Robert W., and Virginia Winslow. 1974. Deviant Reality:
    Alternative World Views. Boston: Allyn and Bacon, chap. 2.

11

THE DIFFERENTIAL PRESSURES TOWARD SCHIZOPHRENIA AND DELINQUENCY

S. Giora Shoham
Lilly Weissbrod
Rachel Markowsky
Yitzhak Stein

It is not schizophrenia but normality that is split-minded;
in schizophrenia the false boundaries are disintegrating.
Schizophrenics are suffering from the truth . . . the ego
being no longer distinct from the object; the subject no
longer distinct from the object; the self and the world were
fused in an inseparable total complex.

Norman O. Brown, Love's Body

INTRODUCTION

The external manifestations of delinquency and schizophrenia
are widely different. However, there is a similarity that begins on
a prior level of analysis, when early socialization is still rather close
to the point of bifurcation into predispositions to social deviance or

The authors wish to acknowledge the role played during the vari-
ous stages of the research by the following: Yitzhaq Aloni, Naomi
Bujikowsky, Rahel Ehrenfeld, Dalia Freiberger, Nava Kaplinsky,
Giora Rahav, Nura Resh, Esther Segal Yaakov Shaked. They also
wish to thank the doctors, and hospital, and prison personnel of the
following: Yehuda Abrabanel Hospital: Dr. O. Haker, Dr. M. Zohar
Be'er Yaakov, Dr. R. Mayer; Beilinson Hospital: Professor Amnon
Fried; Geha Psychiatric Hospital: Professor H. Wysenbeek; Haim
Sheba Medical Centre: Dr. I. Farin, Dr. W. Bodenheimer; Ramla
Central Prison: the director, Elias Darnitchero; Shalvata Hospital:
Dr. Yaffe, Dr. Kalman, Dr. Gaoni; Talbieh Hospital: Dr. Krasilow-
ski.

functional psychoses. First, the etiological schemes themselves are quite similar in their structure. Schizophrenia is believed to develop by a feedback cycle triggered by loss, deprivation, or other personal tragedies in the vulnerable transitory period of the puerperium, or adolescence. However, a predisposition to psychosis, which has crystallized presumably in early childhood, has to be present for the later event to catalyze the onset of schizophrenia. Similarly, in criminology, some hypothesize that a predisposition to delinquency is incurred by a youth growing up in a broken or inadequate family, in neighborhoods of high delinquency rates, and in societies suffering from normative disintegration (anomie). These factors, which ideally should be expressed in probabilistic terms, raise the chances that an individual will be initiated into the life of crime through later dynamic processes of role playing and association (Shoham, 1968).

The similarity becomes striking when we compare some major trends in criminology and the recent theoretical expositions of schizophrenia. The main currents in criminological theory link most of criminal or socially deviant behavior to learning processes (Shaw and McKay, 1942; Sutherland and Cressey, 1970). One may be socialized in some cases by criminal parents, siblings, or even whole communities, such as the Indian criminal tribes. In most cases, however, the learning of criminal and deviant patterns of behavior is preceded by rejection of legal structures and alienation from the prevailing value systems.

As in criminological theory, no physiological correlates have been firmly established as a cause of the functional psychoses. The most we can say is that if there is any etiological link between somatic factors and the functional psychoses, it has not yet been proved to exist.

The significantly high incidence of schizophrenia in families of schizophrenic parents or siblings could quite readily be explained by the transmission of ego defects in early socialization (Giffin, 1960); that is, by the internalization through learning of the parents' faulty patterns of interaction, or even by the general breakdown in communications within a "schizophrenogenic" family (Lidz and Fleck, 1962; Bateson et al., 1956). Similarly, a boy growing up in a criminal family such as the "notorious Jukes" must be very disturbed indeed if he grows up to be a priest or a rabbi.

A seemingly more complicated task would be to replicate to schizophrenia our second major premise, that crime is "normal" behavior. Here again, the statement is more exclusionary than positive, as it aims to deny etiological primacy to structural personality defects.

The normalcy contention means in this context that the difference in personality structure is not physiological and/or hereditary, but an outcome of the socialization process—so personality differences be-

tween delinquents and the rest of the population are differences in degree and not in kind. Likewise, schizophrenia is an extreme condition far removed on the slopes of the normal curve, but by adopting
Harry Stack Sullivan's stance that schizophrenia is not a "disease
entity" but a "grave disorder of living," we are coming close to the
contemporary approaches that regard the functional psychoses as a
breakdown of interaction (Mullahy, 1967).

As has been pointed out elsewhere (Shoham, 1970), all the syn-
dromes of the functional psychoses identified by contemporary psy-
chiatrists have been considered at other times, other places and in
other cultures as normative behavior, fashionable, commendable, or
even as proof of divine visitation. This leads us to a sociocultural
definition of the functional psychoses as a process incidental to inter-
personal communication and interaction, which is labeled as morbid
in a given cultural context (Crowcroft, 1967). This definition would
be in line with the ingenious observation by P. Halmes that, "cultures
vary according to the degree of abnormality they encourage and legiti-
mise" (Halmes, 1957). The societal reaction to a given human condition, and not this condition or behavior per se, define it as morbid for
the individual patient and his relevant others.

The definition of functional psychoses as the dissolution of the
"ego boundary" can fruitfully be linked to the sociocultural explanation of psychosis. We have dealt at length with the formation of this
"ego boundary" and its function as an imaginary dividing line between
our cognitive structure, which synchronizes interaction, and the outside world (Bateson, 1960). This ego boundary is being destroyed in
psychosis. The dissolution here is in a reversed order, where the
outer concentric circles of the ego boundary decay slowly or explode
abruptly. The infantile ego-core remains then to take care of cognitive reality, which it is very poorly equipped to do. In the severe
cases of schizophrenia the ego boundary is completely destroyed and
the patient reverts to early childhood, to the pantheistic oral stage
where no dividing line exists between him and the outside world.

One of our basic theoretical premises relates to two personality
core vectors. These are "participation" and "separation." By participation we mean the identification of ego with a person (persons), an
object or a symbolic construct outside himself, and his striving to
lose his separate identity by fusion with this other object or symbol.
Separation, of course, is the opposite vector. However, as vectors
are multidimensional, the pressures are much more likely to take
place on the different planes of a space, which represents the human
personality, than along a unidimensional continuum. In our use of
these opposing vectors of unification—fusion and separation—isolation
as the main axis of our theory would be in conjunction with the three
major developmental phases. First, the process of birth: this abupt

propulsion from cushioned self-sufficiency into the strife and struggles of life outside the womb is a major crisis, which is recorded undoubtedly by the newborn's psyche. These initiate the opposite vector of participation, which is a directional driving force harnessing a diverse assortment of psychic energy toward union with given objects or symbolics. The fetus at birth is physiologically and psychologically capable of recording these colossal crises incidental to his birth, and he is traumatized by them into a life-long quest for congruity and unification.

The second process of separation is the crystallization of an individual ego by molding of the "ego boundary." The infant shrieks and kicks his way into the world, but he still feels himself part and parcel of his entourage. However, this pantheistic bliss is gradually destroyed by the bumps and grinds he suffers from the harsh realities of hunger, thirst, discomfort, physical violence from hard objects in his surroundings, and a mother who is mostly loving but sometimes nagging, apathetic, hysterical, or overprotective. All this shoves, cajoles, and pushes the infant into coagulating a separate identity: to leave the common fold of unity with his environment and crystallize an "I." This individual self knows then that he is not part of and with everything, but vis-a-vis his surroundings and opposite everybody.

Later on the various demands of the socialization agencies, the necessity to fit into the boundaries of the normative system and to gain one's "ego identity," are the semifinal or the final, as the case may be, separating pressures. After these the individual is on his own, ontologically lonely and trying desperately to regain the togetherness of his lost fold. In this climbing uphill the individual may choose both legitimate and illegitimate paths, both strictly acceptable and deviant avenues.

An attempt to grade the intensity of the participation vectors can be presented in the following decreasing order. First is the reversal of birth, which is the most radical and would be linked, therefore, to the various techniques of unio mystica by the annihilation of the separate self. Second is the dissolution of the ego boundary, which might result in extreme cases in insanity and autistic schizophrenia. Third is the neutralization of the socionormative separation, which might display itself in crime and social deviance. Although our first examples of participation happen to be deviant, most attempts at participation are legitimate and institutionalized.

Our basic assumptions and corresponding set of hypotheses have been that the coagulation of the separate self and ego boundary occur in the symbolic-interaction matrix of the child-mother dyad. The structure of this interaction in the oral stage may be fruitfully represented by the model shown in Figure 11.1, which is basically an intersection of the mother and child axes.

FIGURE 11.1

Mother-Child Interaction in the Oral Stage

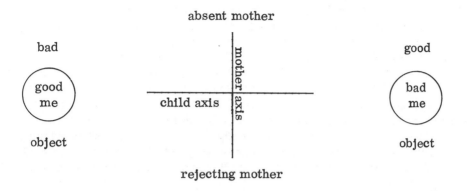

The mother axis has at one extreme the absent mother: the Genet-type foundlings who grew up in institutions with very little care, where the surrogate breast is the nipple of a bottle that is provided erratically and sometimes carelessly, and the surrogate mother is the fleeting image of the passing nurse (Shoham, 1970). The other extreme is represented by the rejecting mother. This includes a wide range of maternal attitudes: from the openly rejecting mother to the frustrating mother who does not fulfill the infant's needs for nourishment and comfort and is consequently perceived by the child as hating and rejecting (Fairbairn, 1966). The indifferent mother is the physically or mentally incapacitated mother or the mother who is overburdened with children and work and is physically present but emotionally tired and detached. Our mother axis represents, of course, a "skewed" and anomalous continuum of maternal attitudes because more or less "normal" maternal care does not predispose the infant to morbidity.

The child axis has on one extreme the negative (bad me) ego boundary, surrounded by the good object (mother). At the very early oral stage described by Freud as primary narcissism, by Fairbairn as "mouth-ego with a breast," and by us as omnipresent pantheism, the mouth feeds (empties) the breast and is temporarily content. However, disturbances in feeding and other related irritations generate the agony of want and pains of anxiety. Consequently, says Fairbairn, the infant infers that this feeding destroyed the nourishing and comforting breast (Fairbairn, 1966). This is not tenable to us. At the

very early oral stage the "mouth entity" is not capable of problem
solving. Moreover, the me/object dichotomy does not yet exist at
this pantheistic stage. Therefore, any pain, anxiety, and want that
occur are in me and only in me because I am omnipresent; and, except the mouth-anchored me, there is nothing. The badness of the
me becomes aggravated by a neglecting mother because, due to lack
of care, the infant is much more likely to experience deprivation,
painful encounters with objects, and such. Consequently, a fixation
at the early oral phase would result in the registration of a painful
wanting (bad) me where the nourishing (good) something is somewhere
in the vague uncharted outside of me, which is, at this stage of
awareness, outside of everything. What is present is a painful ach-
ing me, and the nourishing and soothing goodness that was previously
me is absent out there, hovering evidently out of my reach. An early
oral fixation is therefore a "bad me" surrounded by the good (nourishing) object.

At the other extreme of the child axis of our model we have the
good self surrounded by the bad object (mother). The later oral
stage of development is characterized by a partial differentiation of
the infant from the mother and the development of ambivalence toward
her, which is manifested, inter alia, by the biting of the breasts by
the child in its moment of aggression (Fairbairn, 1966). Here again,
we may add our own observation on the nature of later oral fixations.
The emerging separation of the self due to the deprivational interaction with mother creates an easily accessible source and a sequential
explanation of the frustrations, deprivations, and anxieties of the infant. The noncaring, nonfeeding mother, which is already separate
from the suffering (good) me, is all-apparent and very often in front
of the child's mouth. This location of responsibility is accentuated
by the vengeful bite.

It is necessary at this stage to elucidate further our conception
of developmental fixations. The coagulation of the separate self from
the nondifferentiated pantheism of early orality is effected by the deprivational interaction of the infant with its objects (breast, mother,
its surrogates, and the elements).

In like manner, the separation of the child from the cushioning
and irresponsibility of the family is brought about by the burdens of
socialization and the normative rites of passage into puberty. If
these processes, which are deprivational in essence, are more painful at a given developmental phase than the modal harshness (as
measured by ego's own experience), a rupture, a developmental
wound, is formed, which the psychic energies rush to mend. To be
more precise: we have envisaged the developmental processes as an
interplay between the separating forces of growth and interaction and
the participating urge to revert back to an earlier developmental phase.

However, if the separating effects of the deprivational interaction
were, at a given space-time, too intense or violent, the developmental
process would be temporarily disconnected. The separating injury
blows a fuse and short-circuits the developmental process. The processes of growth and the conflicts with the environment cover the injury with developmental scar tissue, not unlike the scar on a wound.
Yet the wound itself and the tender coats of scar tissue are still exposed to conflict and more pressure because the deprivational interaction of the nascent ego with its entourage is a continuous process.
Consequently, the ever-thickening layers of the scar tissue, which
result from the trauma of the fixation, are more like a corn on a toe.
The cathected energy whirls around the traumatized developmental
area covering it with excessive mental imprints, very much like the
whirls and loops of the skin texture of the corn as it forms a lump
protruding from the texture of the skin. The corn is painful not only
because of the pressure but also because the excessive scar tissue
makes it more vulnerable. Because of the trauma the whole area is
oversensitive. This, on a rather low level of abstraction, illustrates
the nature of fixation. It is a combined outcome of the traumatizing
injury and the excessive and frantic patching of layers of developmental scar tissue. The harsher the trauma the thicker would be the layers of the defensive scar tissue. This should be related to our analysis elsewhere of the formation of the ego boundary. The separate
ego emerges out of the nondifferentiated early orality through its deprivational interaction with its breast-mother and surrounding objects.
The resulting boundary around the self is also a developmental scar
tissue, but a fixation is an overtraumatized developmental experience
that is more conspicuous, more sensitive, and, consequently, more
vulnerable than the rest of the developmental texture of the personality.
     Our present premise, which is, to be sure, hypothetical at this
stage, is linked to solid empirical observations. We have mentioned
Rosenzweig's typology of reactions to frustrations (Shoham and Nehari, 1970b; Rosenzweig, 1962). These are measurable personality
trends, which in their significant form are present throughout an individual's life; and they are believed to crystallize at the oral phase of
development. The intropunitive type, who tends to blame himself for
whatever frustrations and failures he may experience, would be more
the "bad me" individual who has only himself to blame for the disap-
pearance (destruction) of the good object (breast mother). Per contra
the extrapunitive type would be more likely to form when the frustrating mother (object) is tangible out there and may be clearly blamed
for any misfortune and hardship. Consequently, our hypothesis is
that the intropunitive type of personality would be fixated at the early
pantheistic oral stage, whereas the extrapunitive type would be linked
to a later oral fixation when the ego boundary has been coagulated and

separated from its entourage. This is important because our highly
theoretical and conjectural model gets, thereby, an empirical refer-
ent. It should be stressed that at this stage we are still concerned
with the structure of the "skewed" and abnormal mother-child interaction and not with its morbid results.

One of the most controversial of the "skewed" mother-child interactions has been denoted by Bateson and his associates as "double-
binds" and described as follows:

> When the individual is involved in an intense relationship,
> that is, a relationship in which he feels it is vitally impor-
> tant that he discriminate accurately what sort of message
> is being communicated so that he may respond appropriately.
> And the individual is caught in a situation in which the
> other person is expressing two orders of message and one
> of these denies the other. And the individual is unable to
> comment on the messages being expressed to correct his
> discrimination of what order of message to respond.
> (Bateson, 1956)

In a "Review of the Double Bind Theory," Paul Watzlawick (1963)
notes that the bind is a mutual one, binding two parties, two victims.
According to Bowen, the infant and mother enter into a double-bind of
"being for each other," the child "being helpless for the mother" and
the mother "being strong for the child." When the child's self is devoted to "being for the mother," he loses the capacity of "being for
himself" (Bowen, 1960).

Through this symbiotic tie, the mother and child try to perpet-
uate the highly pleasurable stage in both their lives. Any further
development or growth of the child threatens this symbiosis. What
is crucial here is that we attach a different interpretation to this
mother-child attachment: the fixation on early orality might prolong
the pantheistic fusion of child and breast, create a "double-bind"
situation, and arrest or injure "normal" development. However, as
the double-bind situations predispose a person to psychosis, we claim
that this predisposition is related to the abnormal structure of the ego
boundary, which is characteristic of psychoses and which is caused,
among other things, by double-binds. Yet this common denominator
between the double-binds and psychoses is only a particular instance
of the wider texture of participation. If psychosis, with its disruption
of reality and its twisting of cognition, is one of the end products of
ontological participation, the double-bind with its retardation or ham-
pering of the formation of the separating ego boundary and its prolonga-
tion of the child/mother pantheistic union is a forceful technique of
participation, of delaying the expulsion from "Paradise."

Our conception of double-binds is somewhat different from the original one offered by Bateson and Lidz and Fleck in being confined to the family matrix in general, but mainly the very early relationships of mother and child very soon after birth. At this stage, the resentment, or rejection, by the mother of her newly born infant is at its optimal intensity, especially if the mother herself is of the schizophrenogenic type (we adopt this highly controversial connotation for illustrative purposes only, without fully agreeing to the implications of the concept). A postbirth trauma may make both mother and child more vulnerable to the specific type of interaction, which might breed double-binds.

We have denoted as double-bind type A an inconsistent ambiguous and amorphic mother-child interaction where the mother does not know, does not feel, or does not emphasize the needs of the child; where she tends to confuse his needs with hers; where she develops a neurotic proximity with the infant, prolonging thus its early oral feeling of omnipresence. Consequently, a rather blurred, amorphic, and very weak ego boundary would be formed. A special case of this type of double-bind is where the mother tends to react in an oscillating inconsistent manner to the same basic needs and behavior of the infant. This would result in a corrugated, fragmentary, and a brokenly fimbriated ego boundary.

Double-bind of type B would be the one in which cognitive transmissions of acceptance are contradicted by covert transmissions of rejection. In this case the mother would voice and outwardly imitate the conventional gestures of a mother's behavior toward her infant; however, in her immediate attitudes toward him, as expressed by empathy, physical contact, and the other subtle ways of maternal transmissions of attitudes, she would reject the infant and convey to him her own anxieties, which would be translated by the adequately receptive infant as anxieties relating to his own being. At the nondifferentiated state the infant would regard these maternal transmissions as engulfing, sweeping badness that threatens to destroy everything. The resultant ego boundary would tend to be a negative one, filled with the annihilating tendencies toward the mother (breast-object) and the anxiety-laden guilt (badness) of the inadvertent destroyer. A special case of this type of double-bind is scapegoating. In this case, the mother would send messages of rejection toward the child. On the other hand, his being a scapegoat makes him covertly needed as a receptacle for the scapegoating transmissions. This, no doubt, would be the major distinction between the double-bind of type A, where the covert messages of annihilation are contrasted with the mother's cognitive attitude of acceptance, and the scapegoating, where the tags of badness, depersonalization, and rejection conflict with the mother's need to retain the child as a receptacle for her own aggres-

sive and sinister needs. Moreover, this subconscious attitude of rejection would clash with the scapegoating mother's overt gestures of
acceptance, prescribed by her normative role of mother.

ASSUMPTIONS AND HYPOTHESES

Assumptions

Post facto studies are problematic, since they try to reconstruct
some processes in the past by means of research instruments measuring behavior in the present. Some assumptions have to be made, however, to render the sequence of association meaningful in the present
context. The first assumption is that our research instrument is able
to detect some personality differences as well as some peculiarities of
personality structures. The second assumption is that an attitudinal
response to our instrument may be linked to a specific aberration within
the personality structure, that is, to the various forms of schizophrenia
or to social deviance (delinquent and criminal behavior). Our third
assumption is that some traumatic fixations in the early development
of the personality, which are related to morbidity proneness, can be
gleaned by our instrument, which creates hypothetical double-bind
situations. The fourth assumption is that the various conflict situations
during the socialization of delinquents, which are presumably linked
to their deviant behavior, can be gleaned by our instrument, which includes hypothetical situations of normative conflicts.

The simulation device for double-binds used in this research
was a discordance between contents and tone within a single sentence,
that is, a sentence with negative (unpleasant or frightening) contents
was read in a positive (pleasant, gay) tone, and vice versa. This
simulation device was used because of our premise that double-binds
occurred in the early and later oral stages of development. Tone
represents the presymbolic means of communication, which corresponds to the early oral stage; and contents represent the symbolic
means of communication, which corresponds to the later oral stage.

The simulation device used for conflict situations was discordance in the contents of statements within a single sentence (logical
absurdity). This device was used due to our premise that delinquency
is linked to discordant transmissions of norms by the agent(s) of socialization in later stages of development, which are certainly symbolic. Therefore, discordant transmissions of contents would simulate this discordant transmission of norms.

Hypotheses

In view of the above, we would like to propose and test the following hypotheses on four groups of subjects: delinquents, autists, paranoiacs, and a normal control group.

1. Since both delinquency and a normal morbidity are culturally conditioned phenomena, the three groups of delinquents, autists, and paranoiacs will be distinguished from the normal subjects in their reactions to familial situations in which their fixations occurred.

2. Autists will tend to react to tone rather than contents, due to their early oral fixation, which is presymbolic.

3. Autists will tend to relate principally to positive tone (ignoring negative contents), because they conceive the amorphic outside as good, while their "me" is bad. They therefore prefer the positive nonsymbolic stimuli over the negative symbolic one.

4. The perception of autists will be undecided and hazy due to their weak ego boundary.

5. Paranoiacs will tend to be more content-bound than autists due to their later oral fixation, which occurs in the symbolic stage of socialization—but more tone-bound than criminals or normals.

6. Paranoiacs will twist positive contents into negative ones due to their conception of a good "me" surrounded by a bad object.

7. Criminals will be the most aware of conflicting contents due to the conflict situations that were linked to their later delinquent behavior.

8. Both groups of schizophrenics will be more hesitant about their perception of reality than either delinquents or normal subjects because their personality structures are located at either extreme of the normal curve; their ego boundary is either too strong and forms a barrier between them and reality (paranoiacs), or too weak and blurs the distinction between their inner world and reality (autists).

9. Paranoiacs and delinquents will tend to perceive discord in a concordant sentence more than autists or normals due to their conception of a hostile outside world. Paranoiacs will be more extreme in this perception than delinquents.

10. Autists will be hesitant mainly in the conception of discordant sentences, since they perceive the outside world as good (concordant) and they do not know how to cope with discordant outside stimuli, which contradict their preconception.

RESEARCH DESIGN AND METHODOLOGY

Populations Studied

The population studied consisted of four groups of 30 subjects each, comprising normal hospital patients, hospitalized autistic schizophrenics, hospitalized paranoiac schizophrenics, and imprisoned delinquents. Consequently, the entire population was subject to conditions of a total institution to control for the possible influence of this variable. The institutions comprised one general hospital, four mental hospitals, and one prison. The four groups did not constitute statistical random samples but were chosen and diagnosed by the relevant institution authorities according to the following criteria stipulated by us: males, aged 18 to 30, knowledge of Hebrew, institutionalized for at least five days prior to the interview. As for the criminal group we excluded all those sentenced for sexual crimes, traffic offenses, and crimes against the state.

The Measurement Instrument

A battery of 32 sentences was recorded on a tape. Contentwise, 16 of them described unpleasant situations (negative sentences), the other half described peaceful or joyful situations (positive sentences). The sentences were read by a professional actor, who intoned half of each type in a gay voice and half in an angry one. On a second tape the same sentences were read again by the actor, but this time with the opposite intonation. This was done to cancel out any possible bias created by the succession of tone in which the sentences were read. Half the subjects listened to one tape and half to the other.

To measure the spontaneous reaction to the sentences, subjects were required to describe these on four seven-score semantic-differential scales. The scales scored the sentences as running from good to bad, pleasant to repulsive, gentle to cruel, and soothing to frightening. Subjects were asked to mark down their reactions to the sentences heard on the four scales, which were printed on a separate page for each sentence and in alternating succession (to control for set answering patterns). The tape was then played to the subjects a second time, and the latter required to state whether there was a discrepancy between content and tone of reading. This they again marked down on a seven-score semantic-differential scale for each sentence.

The first four scales were intended to measure the differential reaction to transmission of content (symbolic communication) and tone (nonsymbolic communication) of the research groups, when both types of communication were contained in a single sentence. The fifth scale tested the differential perception of this contradition between symbolic and nonsymbolic communication.

In addition, a second tape was played to the subjects containing 19 sentences, 12 of which were logically absurd (contained contradicting statements). Of these 12, five described family conflict situations; four of the logically concordant sentences also described family situations. These sentences were read in a neutral tone of voice. Subjects were required to distinguish between absurd and logical sentences, again on a seven-socre semantic-differential scale. This scale measured the differential perception of logical conflict.

FINDINGS

General

Our data have substantiated the hypothetical distinction between normative conflict within the family context and double-binds. Double-binds were found to be significantly more associated with morbidity, whereas conflict situations within the family were found to be more associated with delinquency. This would mean that prima facie, at least, the whole body of knowledge relating to the double-bind phenomenon has found a partial vindication in our data. It has been argued many times that double-binds are theoretical constructs only, without any anchor in reality. J. Haley and associates of the pioneering Bateson and Lidz studies on the double-bind have sometimes remarked sadly that they could not find any empirical support for the existence of double-bind, or, for that matter, any link of double-binds with the teleological processes of morbidity.

Barring rejection of our assumptions, as well as our methodological techniques, one has to accept the finding of a significant association between morbidity and double-binds, and, by inference at least, the operation of double-bind mechanisms along the chain of causality of the processes of morbidity. Our finding, that in cases of morbidity the conflicts between sound and symbolic communication were more significantly perceived by morbid than by healthy subjects, does indeed support our present premise that double-binds have more significance in the presymbolic stage of communication between mother and child. The various expositions concerning the validity of double-binds as a causal indicator of morbidity should better be taken in conjunction with the claim of the British oralists* as to the feasibility of the double-bind situation interfering with the development of object relationships normally occurring in early orality by interaction of the neonate with his mother.

There have been several empirical studies attempting to verify the link between double-binds and schizophrenia. Two of them, by Loeff and by Mehralian and Wiener, respectively, could not substantiate this link. The research done by Loeff employed a design somewhat similar to ours, yet reached opposite conclusions. Another study is in line with our findings. Bailey has found that children with a predisposition toward morbidity tend to perceive emotional communications more clearly than other types of communications (Bailey, 1972).

Also there is a discrepancy between the tone of the communication and its contents and those with a predisposition toward morbidity tend to perceive the tone more than the contents.

The most conspicuous finding is that the paranoiacs tend to be extremely isolated from the rest of the three groups (normals, delinquents, and autists), which, although distinct from one another, tend to cluster in the same area.

This fits our overall theoretical orientation in rejecting the fourfold taxonomy of Kraeplin (H. F. Ellenberger, 1974) and adopting Sullivan's continuum of the schizophrenics ranging from the outwardly aggressive paranoiac reaction to the more inwardly aggressive other types of schizophrenia (Sullivan, 1953).

This extreme divergence of the paranoiac reaction from that of the other three groups points to the extremity of paranoia as a phenomenon. The positive feedback cycles of paranoia tend to augment, enlarge, and twist all perceptions. Similarly, the paranoiacs were totally unperceptive of conflicts in contents because the psychic dynamism of the paranoiac has probably become so totally different in context from the accepted perception of reality that, within his world of hallucinations, partial contents, which relate to a totally other reality, are either insignificant or trivial.

Deviance, Morbidity, and Crime Within the Family Context

Our second overall finding, which has a direct bearing on a wider theory linking the etiology of crime and morbidity, is the existence of

---

*For convenience's sake, we have adopted the tag of British to the offshoot of psychoanalysis that has been expounded in Britain by Melanie Klein and her disciples.

a common denominator between criminals and schizophrenics as distinguished from normal subjects. The former have a significantly more extreme reaction to items relating to familial interaction. Among the 14 sentences discriminating between normals and criminals, 64 percent describe family situations, whereas the corresponding percentages for the ten sentences discriminating between criminals and paranoiacs on the one hand, and criminals and autists on the other, are 20 and 25, respectively. This means that skewed family situations distinguish well between normals and criminals but do not constitute a distinction between criminals and schizophrenics. Consequently, there is a marked similarity among criminals and schizophrenics as far as skewedness of family relations is concerned.

Concordance and Discordance of Perception Differentiating Between Deviance and Morbidity

Our instruments were designed to measure both reaction and conception of concordance and discordance between tone and contents, as well as conflicts between statements of fact within the contents, irrespective of tone. The various possibilities are as follows:

Tone	Contents	
	Positive	Negative
Positive	Concordant	Discordant
Negative	Discordant	Concordant

The various hypotheses regarding the findings of discordant and concordant perceptions were as follows: the paranoiac predisposition, having been fixated after the object-mother was separated from the self, tends to identify any deprivational interaction with the depriving object. The coagulation of the ego boundary around the self was effected through a violent interaction with the object, the fixation on which is the scar tissue around the self. We could envisage an ego boundary containing a "good me," that is, the vulnerable self being victimized and attacked by a surrounding bad object. These theoretical expositions, initiated by the British oralists and carried further by Shoham, (1975) can be tested in the present context by the perceptual differences between the paranoiacs and the other groups of the various stimuli directed toward them.

Since we have hypothesized that the paranoiac reaction is related to a later oral fixation, in which the object has already been separated from the omnipresent mass of the nascent self, the aggressiveness of the paranoiac reaction is directed toward a bad object. The contents

of the sentences in our context indeed relate to the later stage of development, where symbolic communication (language) is feasible. The
discrete temporal description of objects, which involves the recognition and manipulation of the separate entities that constitute the description of the outside world, is also inherent in the contents of the
sentences and not in the tone. We see, therefore, that the negative
contents of the sentences in our instrument are being accepted by the
paranoiac, whereas he twists the positive contents so that when the
normals react to positive contents, the paranoiacs tend to turn them
into negative ones; and when the contents are bad, they tend to make
them worse. However, in addition to this goal-directed tendency of
the paranoiacs to twist the "good contents" (the good object) into a
bad one, which is in keeping with our basic hypothesis, they also tend
to twist bad stimuli into good ones rather symmetrically, and vice
versa. Despite this twisting effect, the paranoiac self-concpet is as
a "good me" surrounded by a menacing object, toward which he may
divert his aggression. Table 11.1 presents the comparison between
predisposition to paranoia and to delinquency.

The paranoiacs again tend to distort symmetrically whatever
appears to be reality to the delinquents. Relative to delinquents, the
paranoiacs relate to tone in discordant sentences. This is in line with
our general hypothesis, stated earlier, that the delinquents are com-

TABLE 11.1

Reactions to Concordant and Discordant Sentences—Relative
Comparison Between Delinquents and Paranoiacs
(in percent)

Sentences	Delinquents Reaction		Paranoiacs Reaction	
	Nega-tive	Posi-tive	Nega-tive	Posi-tive
Concordant				
Positive	0	100	100	0
Negative	100	0	0	100
Discordant				
Negative content—positive tone	100	0	0	100
Positive content—negative tone	20	80	80	20

Source: Compiled by the author.

pletely content-oriented and they are sensitive to conflicts in contents, because they have been socialized in a conflict-laden environment. The paranoiacs, however, being fixated on the object, are nevertheless still sensitized to the tone; because if the contents-based conflict in the socialization of the delinquent extends throughout adolescence and even later, the paranoiac fixation on the object in later orality is still not far removed from the preceding period when language was not as yet mastered and the child was sensitized to the tone more than to symbolic communications. Moreover, in discordant sentences, the relevant reactions signify the predisposition to paranoia within the matrix of a rejecting mother sending aggressive, nonverbal, intuitive tonal messages toward the infant. Table 11.2 presents the comparison between the reaction to tone and contents by delinquents and autistic schizophrenics.

TABLE 11.2

Reactions to Concordant and Discordant Sentences—Relative
Comparison Between Delinquents and Autists
(in percent)

Sentences	Delinquents Reaction		Autists Reaction	
	Negative	Positive	Negative	Positive
Concordant				
Positive	20	80	80	20
Negative	100	0	0	100
Discordant				
Negative content—positive tone	100	0	0	100
Positive content—negative tone	17	83	83	17

Source: Compiled by the author.

In cases of discordance between bad contents and good tone, delinquents tend to disregard the latter and react to the sentence as a negative stimulus. This is in line with our conception of delinquency as linked to conflicts in the socialization process in the late or postoral stage, when communication is already symbolic and the ego boundary already formed. Perception is then anchored on contents (in symbolic communication), and the object regarded as bad. Predisposition to autism, on the other hand, relates more to the tone of the

communication than to its contents. The intropunitive, early oral–
fixated predisposition to autism anchors itself on the tonal communications that relate to the good outside breast–mother. It should be mentioned that both the delinquents and the autistic schizophrenics tend
to generate concordance out of the discordant sentences; the delinquents toward the bad contents, and the autists toward the good tone.
Needless to say, the delinquents react to the negative concordant sentences realistically, whereas the autists react to them in a totally
inverse manner, that is, they perceive them as having good contents
and good tone. This also is in line with the early oral fixation of the
autists and their intropunitiveness relating goodness to the outside
amorphous environment. The delinquents obviously have no problem
in perceiving aggressive contents as bad when reinforced by an aggressive tone. In similar vein, Table 11.3 presents similar results in
the same direction, in a comparison between normal and autistic
schizophrenics.

　　　This is in line with our previous finding: the normals are content bound, although less so than the delinquents, since the conflict
situations during socialization of delinquents make them more sensitive to conflictual contents. In a sense, this relates to what we have
termed as conflict situation of type 1, in which conflictual presenta-
tions of fact by the socializers are associated with the delinquent solutions of the children (Shoham, 1966).

TABLE 11.3

Reactions to Concordant and Discordant Sentences—Relative
Comparison Between Normals and Autists ·
(in percent)

Sentences	Normals Reaction		Autists Reaction	
	Nega-tive	Posi-tive	Nega-tive	Posi-tive
Concordant				
Positive	25	75	75	25
Negative	86	14	14	86
Discordant				
Negative content—positive tone	86	14	14	86
Positive content—negative tone	0	100	100	0

Source: Compiled by the author.

SCHIZOPHRENIA AND DELINQUENCY

The autistic predisposition, on the other hand, again consistently twists the bad tone into a better one and relatively disregards the bad contents. Finally, Table 11.4 compares normals with delinquents.

TABLE 11.4

Reactions to Concordant and Discordant Sentences—Relative
Comparison Between Normals and Delinquents
(in percent)

Sentences	Normals Reaction		Delinquents Reaction	
	Nega- tive	Posi- tive	Nega- tive	Posi- tive
Concordant				
Positive	40	60	60	40
Negative	34	66	66	34
Discordant				
Negative content—positive tone	40	60	60	40
Positive content—negative tone	40	60	60	40

Source: Compiled by the author.

Here the greater reliance of delinquents on contents is made apparent. Their twisting of perception of contents-based communications to appear as conflictual, and therefore depriving, is significantly greater than in our normal comparison group. This supports our overall differentiation between delinquents, schizophrenics, and normals. Note particularly the delinquent tendency to twist a concordant positive sentence in the negative direction. This is in line with the delinquent's tendency to perceive outside stimuli as conflictual even if they are factually concordant.

The Perception of Discordance and Concordance
of Tone and Contents

Delinquents perceived negative concordant sentences and discordant sentences of negative tone and positive contents as more discordant. This is in line with our general theory of conflict situations and delinquent solutions, according to which the delinquents tend to anchor on negative, depriving, and menacing outside stimuli. And since they anchor more on the contents of the communication, they tend to twist the contents into a negative stimulus, in keeping with their hostile perceptions of the environment.

It is interesting to note that the paranoiacs symmetrically reverse the perception of the criminals. This reversal holds true for

both concordant and discordant sentences. However, the reversal is
more complete in the discordant sentences. This points to the conclusion that delinquents, being extreme in their perception of conflicts in reality, are more attuned to selective perception, that is,
they perceive some conflicting and negative transmissions realistically
but tend to select those that fit their negative attitude toward their environment. The paranoiacs, on the other hand, twist all perceptions
in a nonrealistic manner to fit their delusive conceptions of a totally
menacing world. The paranoiacs tend to reverse the discordant sentences more because their initial fixation on the bad object, which sur-
rounds their "good" self, sensitizes them more to conflictual stimuli
than to concordant ones. The reversal is emphasized because the
paranoiacs are more extreme in their inverted reactions than any other
group.

     These data support our contentions about the underlying pressures
toward crime. We have envisaged two types of double-bind—one in
which some extreme transmissions by the mother or mother-surrogate
are contradicted in a rather consistent way, and generate a conflictual
"Gestalt" between the emerging self and its surrounding object-mother.
These transmissions, which we have described earlier, make for a
very strong ego boundary, which makes one relatively immune to the
incoming conflicting transmissions of reality and lets the delusional
negativistic conviction of the paranoiac reign supreme. The extreme
inversion of incoming stimuli is also supportive of our model, to be
presented later, about the conflict between the "good" me and the rejecting object inherent in the predisposition to paranoia. Per contra,
in the double-bind type B, the autistic reaction has been hypothesized
by us to be generated by a relationship between an absent or neglecting mother-object, so the nascent self does not have a strong ego boundary. It is fixated on predifferentiated early orality, so its relationship with reality is detached. Since this makes for a weak and amorphic relationship with the object, in keeping with our findings, its attitude toward the environment is undecided, erratic, and resigned—
as was bound to be the case. This, indeed, is the typical profile of
the autistic reaction, which is mainly characterized by a detachment
from outer reality and a submerging in an inner reality, which cannot be easily reached or communicated with.

CONCLUSIONS

     The hypotheses listed above have been tentatively verified by
our findings, and our measurement instrument tentatively validated.
The tentativeness of both these conclusions must be emphasized,
since the research populations were relatively small and did not con-

stitute random samples. Therefore, this must be considered a pilot study only, and the results should not be seen as completely conclusive.

Our findings verified the basic hypothesis of a common denominator for both morbid and delinquent subjects, as contrasted with the normal ones, and specifically one related to familial interaction. Morbidity and delinquency were thus shown to be related to breakdowns in the socialization process, rather than "disease entities" of various sorts.

The findings also support our distinction between autism and paranoia as occurring in the early oral and later oral stages of development, respectively, by showing the predominance of tone orientation among autists as contrasted with the contents orientation of paranoiacs. Our postulate of a weak ego boundary of autists, linked to neglect in the early oral phase, which interferes with formation of a perception of the "me" as distinguished from the environment, has been verified by their hesitant reactions and perceptions of discordant situations. In contrast, paranoiacs were shown to have a delusionary conception of the outside world, which supports our postulate of an over-strong ego boundary linked to the deprivational interaction and rejection in the later oral stage. Such a strong ego boundary bars all incoming stimuli from being conceived realistically. We also postulated an aggressive, negative conception of the environment for paranoiacs, which was supported by our findings.

Above all, the validation of our research instrument, which was based on simulation of double-binds, supports the existence of the latter as significantly linked to a predisposition to schizophrenia.

The last hypothesis concerning delinquents was only partially verified by our findings. They were not found to be more sensitive to conflict situations, or else conflicting statements do not simulate conflict situations in the socialization process. In the latter case, our third measurement instrument was not valid.

REFERENCES

Bailey, M. M. 1972. "Vocal and Verbal Communication of Emotion by Parents of Schizophrenic and Non-Psychotic Disturbed Adolescents and Young Adults." Dissertation Abstracts International 32, no. 11 (B): 6633.

Bateson, G. 1960. "Minimal Requirements for a Theory of Schizophrenia." Archives of General Psychiatry 2 (November): 477-91.

Bateson, G., et al. 1956. "Toward a Theory of Schizophrenia." Behavioural Science 1 (October): 251-64.

Bowen, M. 1960. "A Family Concept of Schizophrenia." In Etiology of Schizophrenia, edited by D. D. Jackson. New York: Basic Books.

Crowcroft, A. 1967. The Psychotic. New York: Penguin Books.

Ellenberger, H. F. 1974. "Psychiatry from Ancient to Modern Times." In American Handbook of Psychiatry, edited by S. Arieti. New York: Basic Books.

Fairbairn, R. 1966. Psychoanalytic Studies of the Personality. London: Tavistock.

Giffin, M. E., A. M. Johnson, and E. M. Littin. "The Transmission of Superego-Defects." In The Family, edited by Vogel and Bell. Glencoe, Ill.: Free Press.

Halmes, P. 1957. Towards a Measure of Man. London: Routledge & Kegan Paul.

Lidz, F., and S. Fleck. 1962. "Schizophrenia, Human Integration and the Role of the Family." In Etiology of Schizophrenia, edited by D. D. Jackson. New York: Basic Books.

Mullahy, F. 1967. "Sullivan's Theory of Schizophrenia." International Journal of Psychiatry 4 (December): 492–521.

Rosenzweig, S. 1962. "The Experimental Measurements of Types of Reaction to Frustration." In Explorations in Personality, edited by H. A. Murray. Oxford: Oxford University Press.

Shaw, C. R., and H. B. McKay. 1942. Juvenile Delinquency and Urban Areas. Chicago: University of Chicago Press.

Shoham, S. 1966. Crime and Social Deviation. Chicago: Regnery.

_____. 1968. "Culture Conflict as a Frame of Reference for Research in Criminology and Social Deviance." In Crime and Culture: Essays in Honour of T. Sellin, edited by M. F. Wolfgang. New York: Wiley.

_____. 1970. The Mark of Cain. Jerusalem: Israel University Press.

Shoham, S., and M. Nehari. 1970. "Crime and Madness, Some Related Aspects of Breakdowns of Familial Interaction." Annales Internationales de Criminologie (Paris) 9, no. 1: 71–128.

Sullivan, H. S. 1953. Concepts of Modern Psychiatry. New York: Norton.

Sutherland, E. H., and D. R. Cressey. 1970. Principles of Criminology. Philadelphia: Lippincott.

Watzlawick, P. 1963. "A Review of the Double Bind Theory." Family Process 2 (March): 132–53.

12

PATTERNS OF SOCIAL
RELATIONSHIPS AND
YOUTH CRIME: SOCIAL
INTEGRATION AND PREVENTION
Paul C. Friday
John Halsey

Social scientists today generally agree that youth crime and delinquency are pervasive particularly in urban, industrial, and affluent
societies. It is also recognized that the rates of criminal involvement
are far greater than official reports indicate and that most youthful
offenders do not continue in crime but instead become integrated into
society and lead basically law-abiding lives.

The primary question, then, is what factors or conditions increase both the probability of involvement in criminal acts by youth
and set the conditions under which most youth cease such activity.
The underlying factor in both instances appears to be the degree of integration (involvement, commitment, attachment) by youth to the society as a whole and to conforming norms. Integration is fostered by
interaction—interaction in groups that transmit conforming or deviant
norms and that reinforce one behavioral set or another.

There are five major types of social relationships that play a
key role in socialization and in integrating the individual into the society. These are: (1) kin relationships, including the extended family;
(2) school; (3) community or neighborhood; (4) work; and (5) peer role
relationships not otherwise defined by the four others.

These five kinds of role relationships actually imply others as
well. There are many potential relationships of each type, but for the
purposes at hand it is unimportant to distinguish the relationships but
instead to be concerned with the amount of activity and time spent
across them all. Indeed, it is proposed that the degree of social inte-

---

The theoretical section of this paper relies freely upon Paul C.
Friday and Jerald Hage, "Patterns of Youth Crime in Industrial Society: An Integrated Perspective," Criminology 16 (November 1976).

gration of an individual is determined by the significant relationships one has of each type—kin, school, community, work, and peer—rather than the total number of relationships. In other words, the saliency of a given set of relationships is critical, and saliency is measured by activities.

How does one measure the activity in a role relationship? A pilot research study by Marwell and Hage (1970) found that a number of role relationship variables formed a factor that they called intimacy. Despite its name, all of the variables are behavioral; and those with the highest loadings include: few role partners or occupants; wide variety of activities and locations; relatively high frequency of interaction; considerable knowledge about the role partners; common role sets, that is, the role partners had common third parties (overlap); and, finally, activities were in some respects dovetailed, that is, there was some division of labor or interdependence in the role set.

The general hypothesis, then, becomes that if youth have intimate role relationships of all five types then they are much less likely to be engaged in youth crime. Or to put this another way, as the intimacy declines both within certain types of relationships and across all of them, the youth is less integrated into society and more likely to be involved in various kinds of crime (Friday and Hage, 1976).

Thus, the key is not so much whether a youth is unemployed, is in school, has divorced parents, or lives in a ghetto—although these can be important causes explaining a lack of work, school, family, or community role relationships—but whether he has these relationships at all and how involved he is in them. The more involved one becomes in these relationships the less likely he is to engage in deviant acts, and especially the less likely he is to be involved in major crimes.

The importance of any one type of relationship will vary by age. Certainly, family interaction is first in terms of time, school and peer relationships begin around five and seven years, while community and work interaction will come during the middle teen years. Interestingly, at the point when the probability of engaging in role relationships of all types is maximized, involvement in criminality is lower.

The focus of this chapter will be to look at the societal conditions that differentially affect the development of integrative relationships and to make some suggestions as to possible measures that might facilitate integration during the most crime prone years.

WIDER ORIGIN EFFECTS ON PATTERNS
OF ROLE RELATIONSHIPS

What affects the probability for adolescents to have certain role
relationships? It is important to look for factors that would seem to
create special situations for adolescents in particular, rather than
either children or adults. As youth grow older, their capacities for
role relationships increase. Thus, looking at the normal adolescent,
one would expect the gradual development of role relationships in all
areas: kin, school, community, work, and peer. The question is
what factors might retard this natural growth.

The crux of the explanation lies around the simple observation
that with increasing industrialization there has been a steadily lengthening period of adolescence and an increased isolation of youth from
the diverse role patterns. Subsequently, youth are more likely to
be "under"-integrated. Glaser uses the term adolescent segregation
(1975, p. 30).

This phenomenon appears to be a natural requirement of an affluent, urban, industrial society. As technology increases, the skills
required for economic and social participation in the larger society
also increase. The time between childhood and meaningful, working
adult involvement becomes longer. The years of formal schooling
required before gainful employment have increased. Thus, the steadily increasing period of time before youth, on the average, are employed means that adolescence is becoming longer socially, just as
there is increasing evidence that biologically the maturation period is
becoming shorter. It is the lengthening period of an ill-defined position and status that has made delinquency such a common characteristic of contemporary society (Bloch and Niederhoffer, 1958).

Since the burden for preparing individuals with the increased
skills required for economic participation falls on schools, these institutions become critical in any analysis of criminality. Schools are
caught in a bind between public tax support and accountability in terms
of the products they produce; namely, trained, or at least well-pre-
pared, youth for the labor market. Consequently, schools in industrial societies tend to alienate youth both from the adult authorities
in school and from themselves. Schools are extremely critical institutions; individual self-concepts are formed (or at least reinforced)
here, and future economic opportunities are created. If the student
lacks either innate ability or socially approved motivation, schools
generally bypass him. In earlier eras, alienated youth could leave
school and be absorbed into the vast unskilled and semiskilled labor
force (Downes, 1966, p. 263), but the numbers of such jobs and the
willingness to occupy them, is decreasing (Wattenberg, 1966, p. 9).
In general, adolescents as a social category become systematically

restricted in social participation; they are prohibited from integration in the adult society by virtue of age, talents, and skills (Glaser, 1972, p. 9). Since many youth cannot work, their isolation is increased and, as Coleman (1961, p. 3) has stated, "are cut off from the rest of the society, forced inward toward their own age group, and made to carry out their whole social life with others their own age." The saliency of the peer group is increased, yet the peer group is least likely to be integrative and to develop the necessary commitments to conformity.

Adolescents create their own culture—not a counterculture, but a youth subculture with its own fashion, speech, musical taste, and such. In part, this culture is necessary given the structural constraints against work integration in postindustrial society and the increased alienation at home and school. Likewise, youth—given the lengthening of adolescence—are given the time to create a subculture. Postindustrial society has tended to make fewer and fewer demands on youth, creating perhaps the world's largest leisure class without the wherewithal to utilize it. As Friedenberg (1959, p. 9) states, "Society seemingly asks so little of him (youth), merely that he 'grow up,' finish school, and get on the payroll."

Finally, industrialization and urbanization have affected the development of community relationships by increasing the rate of family mobility. Mobility has destroyed the sense of community; and, as a consequence, youth who are raised in neighborhoods where there is no sense of community lose one opportunity for the development of role relationships. It is important to have a variety of role contacts, particularly across age groups. Yet increasingly in urban areas, adults interact with friends who are scattered throughout the metropolitan area and not with individuals who live in the same building or block. Long-term interest in, and control over, youth by conforming adults outside of the family itself is reduced. Youth themselves are mobile, meeting friends away from home and away from the neighborhood where informal social controls are more likely. Once a certain proportion of the population has developed this postindustrial pattern, one can no longer speak of it as a community as such.

SIGNIFICANCE OF ROLE RELATIONSHIP PATTERNS

What are the consequences of having little intimacy in family, school, work, or community role relationships? What happens when role relationships of the various types are lacking? The saliency of peer group role relationships increases. Not only is the salience increased, but behaviorally the youth spends more time in the group. Indeed, there is little else to do. The peer group becomes more significant to the extent that a youth is isolated from or unable to obtain sufficient reward for conformity in the family, school, or other conforming groups. Karacki and Toby (1962) found a lack of commitment to an adult way of life to be at the root of the delinquency problem. In fact, looking at youth gangs, they found that those who appeared nondelinquent tended to be boys who had changed from the youth culture to adult roles and norms and those who had successfully returned to school or work.

Because of the excessive amounts of time spent in the peer group, its saliency, and the lack of a job and work relationships, both power and status as defined by that group become much more important than would otherwise be. Youth who are unsuccessful in meeting the performance standards of school may often compensate by achieving prestige among peers. Friday (1970) found a strong negative correlation between interaction in the family and interaction with friends, indicating that given a lack of familial relationships, there is a turning to one's peer group.

The role relationship model suggests that if an aggregate of adolescents with few adult role relationships start to interact, they will develop group norms relative to powerlessness and status, exhibiting behavior that proves their identity and success. These norms and sentiments are, in turn, the beliefs that function as the extenuating conditions under which delinquency is permissible (Matza, 1964, p. 59).

Given the dynamics of group interaction in nonintegrated groups, that is, youth peer groups that have little contact with the rest of society, the concern about power and status becomes focal. Youth differentiate between themselves, and they appear to do so on the same criteria as adult groups—wealth and power. This, then, increases the probability of stealing; and, one might add, it can also lead to violence, since gang wars and fights essentially flow from concerns about power and status as well—in this instance, male identity rather than just social prestige. Studies of gang activities in Chicago indicate clearly that the precipitating event of many deviant acts was most frequently a threat to youth power and status (Short and Strodtbeck, 1965, pp. 27–46).

Although many thefts by adolescents may appear on the surface to be nonutilitarian, Friday (1974) found in Sweden that such thefts could be seen to reflect concerns about status. Though unable to compete effectively for power and status in the adult world, adolescents still appear to employ the same general criteria of that world, but define them in their own unique fashion. These criteria are reinforced by the increased materialism and consumption required by advanced industrial societies.

One important way of testing this line of reasoning is to ask what happens when the adolescent becomes involved in meaningful role re-

lationships. Although there is no direct test of this, the model does
conform with another interesting fact about youth crime and juvenile
delinquency: after a peak in mid-adolescence, it declines with increasing age. Cessation of criminal activity most frequently corresponds in time with the development of the responsibilities of marriage,
employment, or in other words, the development of a pattern of role
relationships that foster conformity.

The role relationships perspective also explicates the peculiar
need for adolescent conformity to youth norms. Durkheim talked
about the problem of overcommitment to norms as a characteristic
of altruistic suicide. Paradoxically this appears to be a pattern not
unlike youth crime. With only one role relationship left, this group's
norms and definitions become the most important thing. Its norms
and concerns become central for the adolescent member. He must
prove himself to his peers and will take great risks to do so. Thus,
the influence of the peer group will depend to a marked degree on the
intensiveness of peer group involvement as against other involvements
and commitments. Hirschi suggests that if there is no commitment
(attenuated attachments) to parents, school, or such, an individual
is psychologically more available to engage in sporadic acts of deviance (Hirschi, 1969). Unlike Hirschi (1969, pp. 139-41), who be-
lieves that attachment to peers and attachments to parents are directly
related to each other and that both are inversely related to delinquency,
the role pattern perspective suggests that peer attachments are directly related to delinquent involvement. As the saliency of the peer
group increases so too does the probability of delinquency. This argument is supported by Hindelang's attempt to validate Hirschi's
model. Hindelang (1973, pp. 486-87) supported Hirschi's notion of
attenuated attachments reducing criminality except for peer relationships, which he found to increase the probability of delinquency.

IMPLICATIONS FOR POLICY

Assuming the validity of the role relationships model, the general objective of policy dealing with youth offenders should be to help
establish and maintain positive (conforming) role relationships within
the youth's total pattern of family, school, community, work, and
peer interaction. This would involve increasing the variety of activities and increasing the frequency of those activities. In so doing, the
types of activities and groups should overlap in the sense that family,
school, and community associations should not be totally separate.
Integration is fostered when an individual in interacting with one
role set (such as school) knows individuals from another role set
(such as the community). This tends to increase interdependence and

knowledge of the role partner and, in turn, increases conformity.
The differences between a totally integrated role pattern and an isolated one characterizing many deviant youth today may be seen in
Figure 12.1. As one's role set tends toward either ideal type, the
greater the probability is of either conformity or deviance.

To establish crime prevention policy one must concentrate on
ways in which the isolation or segregation of youth is decreased. This
means, in essence, providing greater opportunities for interaction
across role sets and decreasing the inherent alienation in each set.
Efforts directed toward these two goals would tend to reduce the saliency of peer influence.

In basic terms what is needed are conditions that tend to foster
a positive self-concept, a sense of self-worth, a feeling of meaningful
and responsible participation. If the high crime-prone pattern is family alienation, school alienation, and the lack of work or community
relationships, program efforts should be directed in these areas. It
should be emphasized here that the problem is not seen to be the individual deviant, but the structure in which he finds himself.

Ideally, policy should be directed toward all role sets simultaneously. However, reform can come in stages. Since the most
crime-prone period involves the transition from school to work, the
following are a few suggestions that would tend to reduce the lengthening anomic period for most adolescents in urban, industrial societies.
Many of the underlying principles have been utilized in some countries,
and where they have been tried there appears to be a lower rate of
criminality (Buchholz, 1971). Since the most crime-prone period
appears to be during adolescence, when family, school, and community experiences are most important, the thrust of the remaining discussion will concern a redefinition and reorganization of schools.

REDEFINITION AND REORGANIZATION OF SCHOOLS

If integration into society and commitment to conformity is to
be maximized, it is necessary that schools redefine their goals and
enlarge the scope of their education. As a primary socializing agent,
school can have a positive or negative impact on the lives of youth.
At its best, it can work to counteract a harmful family situation. At
its worst, it can act as a stumbling block for those who have had a
positive upbringing. In addition to traditional goals such as the socialization of the student, preparation of future economic roles, and
personality development, the schools could be the first agencies with
which to work toward prevention of delinquency. If we assumed teachers learn more about youth than other agents of social control, such
as welfare workers, police, or court personnel, and if such knowl-

FIGURE 12.1

Integrated and Nonintegrated Role Patterns

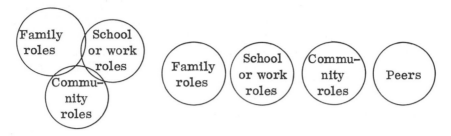

INTEGRATED SET   UNINTEGRATED SET

Source: Compiled by the authors.

edge were used effectively, schools could have a big impact on delinquency. The following suggestions describe how schools and teachers
could be used effectively to provide services within a community.
The primary goal of the reorganization of schools is to encourage the
formation of positive school role relationships between a child and a
teacher, an administrator, or other students, as well as to provide
the opportunity to create overlapping relationships between the school,
family, and community. In short, schools should work toward increasing the cohesiveness of communities and neighborhoods.

The first step to be taken is to make education more individually
oriented as much as possible. In other words, a youth in a class
should be competing more with himself than with other children.
Achievement should center on an individual's progress in relationship
to himself as opposed to others in the class. This is particularly important for low-achievers. Such an innovation would allow all children to achieve in school according to their abilities and decrease
the development of negative self-concepts as a result of failure in relation to other students, reduce unproductive competition, and increase
the potential of positive relationships between student and teacher.
Studies have shown that low achievement in school is directly related
to delinquent behavior (Empey and Lubeck, 1971, p. 82; Gold, 1963,
p. 121; Polk and Schafer, 1972; Reckless and Dinitz, 1972). Low
achievers are prone to feel as outsiders, which, in turn, can decrease
the probability of intimate role relationships within the school (Olofsson, 1971). Thus, failure in school effectively decreases the possibility of formation of positive school role relationships because it causes
students to be alienated with school and all connected with it.

In fact, when Hirschi (1969, pp. 131–32, 156) assessed the independent effect of each variable in his study, he found that liking
school proved more closely associated with nondelinquency than either
communication with father or liking teachers, and this was almost as
closely associated with nondelinquency as a low number of delinquent
friends. Such research implies that as the average duration of school
is increased, a closer relationship has developed between lack of gratification in the school experience and adolescent crime rates (Glaser,
1975, p. 45).

The second step to be taken within schools is to end tracking
systems, which classify students according to their abilities. Tracking, in a sense, establishes a class system within a school. The
ability and behavior of a child are to a certain extent determined by
his social background and family class position. The school, on the
other hand, represents middle–class values; and it is on these that
students are evaluated (Brusten, 1974). Middle–class values carry
with them certain expectations of those from lower social classes,
that is, teachers might expect lower–class youth to underachieve and
exhibit deviant behavior (Hackler, 1971; Brusten, 1974). The result
is that youth from lower social classes will end up in lower tracks,
which provide fewer opportunities for achievement. Those in lower
tracks are likely to perceive themselves as underachievers. This has
a large impact on the self–concepts of students in these tracks. It is
also likely that such tracking systems disrupt the possibility of positive role relationships among students because, in effect, it fragments
the student body, making it difficult for integration to occur.

Third, in addition to eliminating tracking, schools need to redefine the priorities of education. University or theoretical training is
not appropriate for all students; yet, frequently, those whose interests
are more practical, manual, or clerical are often treated as "second
class" students. This reduces the positive experience of school and
even reduces the perception of school as "necessary" for these youth.
These are the youth who frequently "drop out" and become the most
crime–prone. The school needs, therefore, to reexamine its status
hierarchy and provide more meaningful input to these pupils. The
school must make more of a commitment to those whose interests do
not coincide with those of university–bound students.

The fourth step to be taken is to involve the community at large
in the school to a greater extent. The importance of this is that involvement of community in school could counteract the effects of urban
living, for it provides a base from which a community or neighborhood
consciousness could develop. An experiment along these lines has
been tried in Colorado (Colorado Youth Services, 1975).

Such an effort could provide a smooth introduction into voluntary
organizations, political organizations, and community action projects.

Such programs have been relatively successful in the Soviet Union, for example, with the Young Pioneers or in the United States with the Boy Scouts. By increasing the scope of possible community activities one increases the probability of creating positive (integrative) role sets. If nothing else, such activities occupy that tremendous amount of unstructured leisure. Such activities geared toward positive, constructive communal goals can provide a sense of responsibility, value, and contribution to the communal good. It is a mechanism of creating a sense of collective conscience, the antithesis of the self-serving individualism fostered by the present structure.

There are many ways in which the community could be more involved in the school. First, education should include community studies in which representatives from various parts of the community would be able to interact with students and explain their roles in society. Police, judges, lawyers, employers, or workers would participate in such studies. This would increase the probability that youth would have community role relationships. At present, schools are generally isolated from the community at large. At a time when adolescents are denied a meaningful position within the society (Friday and Hage, 1976) such efforts could help integrate youth more with the community by providing greater interaction and identification with the positive role models. Second, the school should encourage the community to use its facilities for community events and could sponsor a wide range of activities designed to integrate the family, community, and students. Activities could include recreation programs and social events (dances, discussions, concerts, and the like) aimed not only at students but also at the community at large. Such activities could have an impact on integration of community (Clinard and Abbott, 1973). Third, families and community people should take part in the actual education of youth. Parents and elderly people could be used as teacher aides on a volunteer or paid basis. If more people were used in such a way, students would be more apt to get the attention needed to achieve in school. This would also provide work for those who are unemployed in the community at large while simultaneously providing an overlap of age group relationships reducing youth isolation. Fourth, there should be joint classes for parents and children. Some education could perhaps be shifted to evenings so parents and children could attend school together. Some classes could focus on family relations, community services, politics, or such. This would be a useful way of integrating the family with the school and would perhaps have an effect on parents' attitudes toward education and school. It has been shown that when parents have poor attitudes toward school and the importance of achieving, there is a higher probability that their children will be delinquent (Bachy et al., 1972).

Delinquency has been said to be affected by adolescent unemployment. Modern societies have extended the period of adolescence, thereby isolating the individual from the working world. The idea of the fifth step is to counteract the isolation of the student by incorporating work into education at an early age. Youth should have the opportunity to work in a variety of different occupations so they will have a smoother transition from school to the working world. The value of such experience is that it could foster the establishment of positive work role relationships at an earlier age, thereby counteracting the effects of strong peer role relationships or lack of intimate family role relationships. Work experience should begin with youth between the ages of 13 and 15, as this is the peak age of delinquent behavior (Sveri, 1966, p. 20). Commitments would be created by the training period as well as a reduction in the feeling of worthlessness created by alienation from the traditional theoretically oriented school situation.

The sixth step to be taken is to incorporate social workers and some social services into all schools. Schools can be used efficiently to identify problems of students with family, school, peers, and the like. In this way, it would be possible for social workers to detect problems early and to work toward solutions long before other agencies would be aware of them. It is important that the social workers be integrated into all activities of schools described above. In other words, they should be involved in teaching, recreation, and work experience programs—not simply occupy an office where "problem" children are sent after teachers can no longer cope.

This would increase the social worker's ability to identify problems as well as to provide special services without a stigma or label being attached to those receiving assistance. The impact of labeling is critical to one's self-concept. If one is viewed by others as a problem child, it may not be long before one views himself in a similar way. Thus, it is important that the services to a child be provided in a subtle manner.

The seventh step is to involve students in the actual operation of the school to a larger extent than at present. Too often youth see themselves as being immersed in an educational system that is beyond their control and unresponsive to their needs. This does little to increase a youth's probability of maintaining or desiring positive school role relationships with administrators or teachers. Student governments as they exist today are little more than clubs charged with the execution of relatively meaningless chores, as compared with the work of school administrations. As the length of schooling has increased, so, too, has the need to extend the students' responsibility and participation in the operation of schools. The ages at which this is most important fall between 12 and 18; the older the students, the more important their involvement.

LOCAL SOCIAL SERVICES

As our society has become more industrialized and complex, the problems facing individuals and families have increased. Society has responded by creating a large number of institutions and services to meet the needs of an increasingly complicated existence. Often these services prove to be ineffective and subject to the suspicion of those who need the services most. There are many reasons for this, but for the purposes of this chapter it is interesting to focus on two. First, the services provided to people leave little room for personal initiative and self-respect. Services are provided to people rather than with people. Second, most official service agencies are viewed as being a part of the "power structure," which is beyond the control of the average citizen; and thus, the agencies become the objects of scorn. Social workers and probation workers are often met with the distrust of their clients. This makes it difficult for positive community role relationships to develop.

If social services are to become more effective, a great deal of change must take place. One important reform would be to recognize the value of informal solutions to social problems. Instead of creating many official, specialized agencies to deal with families and individuals, stress should be put on providing people with the means of helping themselves.—Local communities and neighborhoods should take more of the burden and responsibility for local problems. One way to increase informal services would be to encourage local governments to provide incentive funds to local residents. Monies could be provided to those who can demonstrate that they can meet a need within the community and that they are capable of organizing themselves. The role of the local government in the process would be that of providing technical aids and support to those attempting to organize themselves. Such incentive funds would encourage cooperation and a feeling of involvement in solving problems.

Another important reform has to do with the reorganization of formal social services on the local level. It has already been suggested that a number of social services be integrated into the schools. It is now suggested that the administration of all such services be organized within school districts. The actual organization of this would differ depending on location. For example, in cities it might prove effective to use elementary school districts as the basis of services, whereas in small towns, the local school districts would be sufficient.

Coordinating services in this way has many potential benefits. First, the social services would be more responsive to the problems characteristic to such a small area; one would hope that this would result in better services. Second, caseloads would consist of local people, and communication would be facilitated and services more ac-

cessible. Such a system would encourage positive community role relationships as long as services are well run. Third, organization on
a local level encourages local control; there is accountability. To en-
sure this, social workers should be local residents, and administrators
of services should be locally elected. Involvement in local organizations increases integration (Clinard and Abbott, 1974), thereby reducing the probability of crime. Fourth, having services within school districts enables the school and service agency to coordinate activities.
It enables teachers to have important input toward the solution of
problems.

One of the most important services to be provided is family
counseling. The purpose of this service would be to promote positive
family role relationships between a child and his parents. Counseling
would be available for solving parental disputes, child-parent disputes,
and other issues concerning the family. The service would provide
information on child development, birth control, and other related mat-
ters.

The need for services of this kind has been demonstrated. In a
number of studies, it has been shown that various family factors increase the probabilities of delinquent behavior. First, youth with an
upbringing characterized by a lack of supervision and care, inconsistent demands and punishment, and erratic behavior by parents,
have a high probability of being delinquent (S O.U., 1973, p. 25).
Second, youth who have bad relationships with their parents have a
high probability of being delinquent (Hindelang, 1973; Hirschi, 1969;
Olofsson, 1971). These factors hinder the maintenance of intimate
family role relationships. The result is that youth will depend more
on peer role relationships; and, as suggested above, the probability
of deviance is greater if these are the only or predominant kind of
role relationships of a youth.

ADDITIONAL PROGRAMS

In addition to changes within the school and the introduction of
school services, there are a number of other programs that could be
established to meet additional needs in the community. Since the
school is a natural center, programs should be coordinated through it.

One program is the development and coordination of day care
services. They should be staffed with specially trained teachers and
social workers. As more women join the work force, the need for
such facilities has increased. Usually, day care centers are separate
from schools. However, coordination between schools and day care
centers would be useful for a number of reasons. First, social workers could detect developmental problems at a very early age and coor-

dinate needed services with the social workers in the schools. Second, older students could be integrated into the day care programs as part of work experience and to provide them with some sense of responsibility. This would involve them in a community service, and as such, would establish community role relationships.

The impact of early child care on young children could be beneficial. It would mean that other types of role relationships would be possible at a much earlier age. It would provide a greater variety of possible role models. In cases in which family role relationships are unsatisfactory, intimate role relationships of other kinds could counteract negative factors in a child's development. The more varied and diverse the intimate role relationships, the less the possibility of delinquency.

— Another program to be established in the community is a system of recreational facilities (community centers, youth centers, and such) located within the school as well as other parts of the community. In places where these currently exist, their functions need to be extended. The recreation should be aimed at everyone (all age groups) in the community, with special attention given to preteenagers. Part of the problem of youth crime is boredom; the provision of activities for them would clearly function as a diversion. The scope and variety of programs must vary, leaving open the possibility of limited structure; but it would help to have some place to go where the possibility exists of some supervision. A very important factor in the success of recreational activities and centers concerns the involvement of all in the decision-making process. In the case of youth, it is they who should determine what activities are offered. Youth, in particular, should be given greater responsibility in the maintenance of centers. Every effort should be made to increase local residents' involvement and responsibility in such activities.

— A specific aim of the recreation centers is to help establish intimate role relationships of all kinds for youth. It would strive to integrate peer groups and gangs into its activities. It has been suggested that youth with high interaction among peers exclusively are likely to engage in delinquent acts more so than those who interact with many segments of the community.

While reutilization and redefinition of schools can provide the basis for increasing the probabilities of integration for youth, this is not the final solution to the problem of isolated youth and youth crime. What is needed are more basic changes in the nature of the policital economy, for as the role relationships model suggests, the isolation of youth is a natural process of the Western capitalist industrial structure.

What is also needed is the possibility of integrating youth into positions of responsibility and status by providing early apprenticeship programs and, in fact, possibly lowering the minimum age for leaving school. Certainly controls must be placed in the work place to avoid the tragedy of exploiting children, as occurred during the early stages of the Industrial Revolution. But the principle remains: work relationships tend to be integrative since they provide both a sense of responsibility and economic independence; they should, therefore, be encouraged and not discouraged.

Finally, the ultimate course of action requires a redefinition of status. Excessive materialism and conspicuous consumption are clearly a part of the youth crime phenomenon. Youth use the same criteria of wealth and power as the wider society and will be involved in crimes to define a status where one appears to be nebulous. Materialism and consumption are integral parts of many economies today, and when this is coupled with the rhetoric of individualism the consequences are higher rates of property crime. We have no specific recommendations to change the present artificial status structure. We can only hope that in the development of a consumer economy in other societies conscious efforts will exist to define status in terms of personal attributes and not personal property.

The emphasis on property for status is symbolic of a lack of social interaction and integration. When integrative and intimate role relationships are present, status becomes redefined to a more personal level rather than the superficial presentation of self through property. Perhaps the negative effects of materialism will take care of themselves if the social policy becomes one of encouraging greater overlap of interaction between kin, school, community, work, and peer relationships.

SUMMARY

In essence, this chapter has attempted to argue that youth crime is a product of poor integrative mechanisms in the society. It has stated that integration is maximized by the development of positive (intimate) role relationships within kin, school, community, work, and peer group. Maximum integration and subsequent commitments to conformity occur when there is a variety of activities in each group, a high frequency of interaction, an overlap between groups, and an interdependence created on all groups. The extent to which a youth is alienated from any one group increases the probability that a greater reliance will be placed on the peer group for the definition of status and self-worth.

We conclude by suggesting redefinition and reutilization of schools in the community to facilitate the overlap of role relationships between the various kinds of groups. Certainly these ideas are not exhaustive. What is important is that the general tendency to isolate and segregate youth must be changed. This will require a conscious policy; it will not occur by itself. The suggestions included in this chapter are designed to increase the cohesiveness of local communities, thereby increasing the possibilities of youth to maintain positive role relationships of all types—family, school, community, work, and peer.

REFERENCES

Bachy, Duner. 1972. The Role of the School in the Prevention of Juvenile Delinquency. Strausborg: Council of Europe.

Bloch, Herbert A., and Arthur Niederhoffer. 1958. The Gang: A Study of Adolescent Behavior. New York: Philosophical Library.

Brusten, Manfred. 1974. "Soziale Schichtung, selbstberichtete Delinquenz und Prozesse der Stigmatisierung in der Schule." Kriminologisches Journal 6 (January): 29–46.

Buchholz, Erich, Richard Hartman, John Lekschas, and Gerhard Stiller. 1971. Sozialistische Kriminologie. Berlin: Staatsverlag der DDR.

Clinard, Marshall B., and Daniel J. Abbott. 1973. Crime in Developing Countries. New York: Wiley.

Coleman, James S. 1961. The Adolescent Society. Glencoe, Ill.: Free Press.

Colorado Youth Services Institute. 1975. Project Intercept: Delinquency Prevention That Works. Denver: Paul D. Knott.

Downes, David. 1966. The Delinquent Solution. New York: Free Press.

Empey, L. T., and S. G. Lubeck. 1971. Explaining Delinquency. Lexington, Mass.: D.C. Heath.

Friday, Paul C. 1970. "Differential Opportunity and Differential Association in Sweden." Unpublished Ph.D. dissertation, University of Wisconsin, Madison.

158 YOUTH CRIME AND JUVENILE JUSTICE

_____. 1972. "La verifica delle teoric della struttura differenziale delle opportunity delle associazioni differenziali nella societa Svedese." [The applicability of differential opportunity and differential association theory in Sweden] Quaderni di Criminologia Clinica 14 (September): 279–304.

_____. 1974. "Research on Youth Crime in Sweden: Some Problems in Methodology." Scandinavian Studies 46 (Winter): 20–30.

Friday, Paul C., and Jerald Hage. 1976. "Patterns of Youth Crime in Industrial Society: An Integrated Perspective." Criminology 16 (November): 347–68.

Friedenberg, Edgar Z. 1959. The Vanishing Adolescent. New York: Dell.

Glaser, Daniel. 1972. Adult Crime and Social Policy. Englewood Cliffs, N.J.: Prentice-Hall.

_____. 1975. Strategic Criminal Justice Planning. Washington: National Institute of Mental Health.

Gold, Martin. 1963. Status Forces in Delinquent Boys. Ann Arbor, Mich.: University of Michigan Institute of Social Research.

Hackler, James C. 1971. "A Development Theory of Delinquency." The Canadian Review of Sociology and Anthropology 8 (May): 61–75.

Hindelang, Michael J. 1973. "Causes of Delinquency: A Partial Replication and Extension." Social Problems 20 (Spring): 471–87.

Hirschi, Travis. 1969. Causes of Delinquency. Berkeley: University of California Press.

Karachi, L., and J. Toby. 1962. "The Uncommitted Adolescent: Candidate for Gang Socialization." Sociological Inquiry 32 (Spring): 203–15.

Marwell, Gerald, and Jerald Hage. 1970. "The Organization of Role Relationships: A Systematic Description." American Sociological Review 35 (October): 884–900.

Matza, David. 1964. Delinquency and Drift. New York: Wiley.

Olofsson, Birgitta. 1971. <u>Vad var det vi sa!</u> Stockholm: Utbildnings-forlaget.

Reckless, Walter C., and Simon Dinitz. 1972. <u>The Prevention of Juvenile Delinquency</u>. Columbus, Ohio: Ohio State University Press.

Short, James F., Jr., and Fred L. Strodtbeck. 1965. <u>Group Processes and Gang Delinquency</u>. Chicago: University of Chicago Press.

S.O.U. (Statens Offentliga Utredningar). 1973. "Unga lagovertradare IV." No. 49. Stockholm: Department of Justice.

Sveri, Knut. 1966. <u>Kriminaliteten och Samhället</u>. Stockholm: Aldus/Bonniers.

Wattenberg, William. 1966. "Review of Trends." In <u>Social Deviancy Among Youth</u>, edited by W. Wattenberg. Chicago: University of Chicago Press.

THE BALANCE OF SOCIAL STATUS
GROUPINGS WITHIN SCHOOLS AS
AN INFLUENCING VARIABLE ON THE
FREQUENCY AND CHARACTER OF
DELINQUENT BEHAVIOR

Peter C. Kratcoski
John E. Kratcoski

INTRODUCTION

Theories that propose a relationship between social class and
delinquent behavior are common in sociological literature. The underlying assumption in these theories is that individuals internalize a
set of core values and closely adhere to these in their behavior.

There appears to be some disagreement in the literature regarding the role values play in the etiology of illegal behavior among
juveniles. Cloward and Ohlin (1960) have linked juvenile delinquency
with the pursuit of common "middle-class" goals in the American
culture by "lower-class" youths through illegitimate means. This avenue becomes a necessity because of a lack of opportunity in legitimate
modes of behavior for these youths.

Cohen (1955) contended that working-class youths who cannot
gain status in the middle-class goal system often turn to delinquency
to win status and recognition. However, Miller (1958) viewed juvenile
delinquency as more a response to lower-class focal concerns than to
blocked middle-class aspirations. He saw the pursuit of "focal concerns" such as trouble, toughness, smartness, excitement, fate, and
autonomy as having implications for delinquent behavior among lower-
class youth.

Several researchers have downplayed the importance of value
and goal orientations alone in the etiology of delinquent behavior among
youths and emphasized that consideration must be given to the specific
social, cultural, and demographic variables characteristic of the
youths being studied. Such factors as type of community, age, and
peer groups not only play a significant part in the formulation of values
and goal orientations, but also are important in establishing the climate or atmosphere in which a youth operates in his daily life.

Clark and Wenninger (1963) found that locality and the "quality" of the delinquent act, as well as social class, were important considerations when attempting to understand delinquent behavior. They stated,

The pattern of illegal behavior within small communities or within "status areas" of a large metropolitan center is determined by the predominant class of that area. . . . There are community-wide norms which are related to illegal behavior and to which juveniles adhere regardless of their social origins.

Although the juveniles in all communities admitted indulgence in several nuisance offenses at almost equal rates, serious offenses are much more likely to have been committed by lower class urban youths. (p. 58)

Reiss and Rhodes (1961, p. 60) found that the residential area in which a youth lives was highly determinate of his chances for delinquent behavior. They concluded that, "Delinquency life chances of a boy in any ascribed status position . . . vary with the delinquency rate of the residential area."

Although Hirschi (1969) found no significant difference between social class and the rate of delinquent behavior, he did not want this to be construed as showing that social class is unimportant to delinquency. He noted that social class can create differences in rewards, even though the attributes of two competing individuals are equal, and can also create differences in punishment where none exists in obedience to rules.

THE PRESENT STUDY

This study was designed to explore the relationship among stated value orientations, status groupings, and delinquent behavior. The assumption was that the degree of acceptance of a middle-class or lower-class value orientation would not only vary by status group but would be influenced by the proportion of associates with whom the individual interacts who fall within the same social class position. Thus, the individual who falls within a lower or working-class status position, but who lives and goes to school in a predominantly middle-class neighborhood, will follow a value orientation and behavior patterns that are characteristic of that neighborhood and school system of which the student is a part. Conversely, the middle-class individual whose residency and participation in a school system happens to be "lower or working status" will follow the value orientations and behavior patterns of his predominantly lower or working status peers.

Since the adolescent spends a significant proportion of the day in school and generally chooses close friends from school peers, the school climate and peer orientations should be important variables to consider when attempting to understand youthful behavior patterns.

Methodology and Sample

To explore the question of the relationships among value orientation, status grouping, and delinquent behavior, an instrument was developed and administered to a sample of high school students and a sample of institutionalized delinquents. The school sample included a total of 248 cases, gathered from the eleventh and twelfth grades of three public high schools. Selected teachers who were willing to cooperate with the research project were asked to distribute the questionnaires to their classes. The students were informed that participation was voluntary and were told not to identify themselves in any way on the completed questionnaires. The students in the sample were selected from various academic tracks to assure adequate representation.

A sample of 107 males ranging in age from 16 to 18 was selected from an institution for delinquent youths. The same questionnaire administered to the high school sample was given to this group. The self-reported delinquency questionnaire contained information on the youth's background, race, sex, father's occupation, place of residence, acceptance of middle-class and lower-class values, and delinquent behavior. A delinquency checklist taken from Short and Nye (1958) was utilized, with several modifications to take into account local conditions and currently prevalent areas of delinquent behavior.

Value orientations were defined as values, goals, standards, or focal concerns, characterized by Robin Williams (1970) as "major value orientations of America," by Walter Miller (1958) as "lower class focal concerns," and by Albert Cohen (1955) as "middle class standards."

The questionnaire items, many of which were used in the 1963 Clark and Wenninger research, were pretested before the questionnaire was administered. The items were randomly distributed in the questionnaire to try to prevent the students from detecting a pattern and answering accordingly. They were asked to respond to these items by stating the importance each had for them personally, with "great importance," "some importance," and "little or no importance" responses available.

The sample was also divided into status groupings. In the questionnaire, the respondents were asked to indicate specifically their father's occupation. These occupations were ranked and categorized,

using the North-Hatt Occupational Prestige Scale (1961) as modified
by Akers (1961), using the class divisions made by Reiss (1965).
Those who fell within the ranks of one to 59 on the North-Hatt Scale
as used by Reiss were classified as "upper and middle" status. Those
who ranked from 60 to 90 on the North-Hatt Scale were placed in the
"lower and working" status category. Table 13.1 reports the occupational breakdown of the heads of the households for the youths in the
sample at each school.

Analysis and Findings

It was assumed that the students whose parents were predominantly middle class would also come from middle-class neighborhoods,
since the school systems tend to follow the same segregation patterns
by social class as neighborhoods. It was expected that each school
population would reflect the character of the neighborhood from which
the youths came and be predominantly either middle class or working
class in composition. However, an analysis of the census tracts
that the schools encompassed did not totally substantiate this assumption. Based on an analysis of occupation, income, and education of
the populations from which the students in Schools I and II were gathered, the majority was middle class, but there was also a substantial "working class" and even some poverty level representation.

As shown in Table 13.2, the status classification of the students
in the four schools into either "lower and working" status or "middle
and upper" status, using the North-Hatt Scale with Akers' and Reiss'
revisions, revealed that Schools I and II had an almost equal division.
School I is located in a city of approximately 35,000 population. It is
the only high school for that community and draws students from all
socioeconomic statuses. School II is located in a city of 30,000 to
35,000 population close to a large city. Many of the residents of this
community work in other areas. This school is the only high school
for the community. The student population of School III was drawn
from inner-city neighborhoods of a large industrial city. Seventy-
five percent of the students in the sample fell into the lower-working
status group. The students in the institutional sample tended to come
from inner-city areas of the major large cities of the state. Ninety
percent of this sample fell into the lower- and working-class status.

The mean score on the items measuring the importance attached
to middle-class values was tabulated for each respondent. According
to the theories of Merton and Cloward and Ohlin, we would expect
all status groups to have similar value orientations and goals. We
would also expect to find more delinquency among those in the "lower
and working" status group, because of their lack of opportunity to realize these goals through legitimate channels.

TABLE 13.1

Occupations of Youths' Heads of Households
(by school)

School		Unem- ployed	Un- skilled	Semi- skilled	Skilled	White Collar	Profes- sional	Unclas- sified*
					Occupations			
School I								
	Percent	2	10	33	11	30	14	0
	Number	2	10	34	11	31	14	0
School II								
	Percent	0	12	42	25	16	5	0
	Number	0	12	40	24	15	5	0
School III								
	Percent	0	23	46	17	11	3	0
	Number	0	8	16	6	4	1	0
Institution								
	Percent	10	17	39	6	3	1	24
	Number	11	18	42	7	3	1	25

*Those in the "unclassified" category include those heads of households who are on Social Security or wel-fare, deceased, or for whom the youth was unaware of the source of income.

Source: Compiled by the authors.

164

TABLE 13.2

Youths' Class Status
(by school)

| School | Status Grouping | |
	Lower and Working	Middle and Upper
School I		
Percent	46	54
Number	46	56
School II		
Percent	56	44
Number	57	44
School III		
Percent	75	25
Number	33	11
Institution		
Percent	90*	10
Number	96	11

*Twenty heads of households who were on social security or welfare were placed in this category. Six of the youths in the institution sample were unaware of the sources of income of the head of their household. Since these youths had no recollection of the head of the household holding employment, they were also placed in the "lower and working" status.

Source: Compiled by the authors.

The questionnaire contained 15 items reflecting a middle-class value orientation. The possible range of scores was from 15 to 45. A high total score would indicate strong acceptance of middle-class values, a lower score less acceptance.

As shown in Table 13.3, the mean score for acceptance of middle-class values stood at the midpoint (30) or slightly above for both status groups in all four samples, indicating a relatively strong commitment to these values among all the youths. This finding conforms to the theories of Merton and Cloward and Ohlin that regardless of an individual's class position he is drawn toward the middle-class value system. The only difference in the acceptance of the middle-class value orientation appeared in the "lower and working" status group in School III. Their mean acceptance score was approximately five points lower than all other status groupings. It is noteworthy that the

TABLE 13.3

Acceptance of Middle-Class Value Orientation
(mean scores)

School	Status Grouping	
	Lower and Working	Middle and Upper
School I	35.93	36.01
School II	34.63	34.79
School III	30.12	35.90
Institution	36.45	34.54

Source: Compiled by the authors.

"lower and working" status group within the institution did not differ
from the norm on acceptance of middle-class values.

The range of possible scores on the lower-class value orientation scale was from a low of 12 to a high of 36. The mean score for
acceptance of lower-class values stood above the midpoint (24) at all
the schools, indicating that both lower and working status and middle
and upper status youths placed some importance on these values. No
group emerged as placing high importance on these values.

It would appear from these findings that most of the students at
the four schools in the sample, regardless of their status grouping,
embraced a number of middle-class values, such as "being a success,
working hard, staying out of trouble, and having material things,"
and also supported such lower-class values as "having fun and excite-

TABLE 13.4

Acceptance of Lower-Class Value Orientation
(mean scores)

School	Status Grouping	
	Lower and Working	Middle and Upper
School I	25.81	27.01
School II	25.73	25.31
School III	26.21	28.45
Institution	26.87	26.32

Source: Compiled by the authors.

ment, being good at physical activities, taking chances, having freedom, and relying on peer pressures." Perhaps the dissemination of
both sets of values through the mass media and in the school system
is responsible for this mixture of values.

As mentioned in the related research, one would expect to find
a higher rate of delinquency among the "lower and working status"
youths than among the "upper and middle status" youths, either as
a response to lower-class value orientations or as a result of their
inability to obtain and achieve the middle-class standards that they
embrace. To explore this theory, the mean number of illegal acts
reported by the youths in each school and in each status group was
determined.

Table 13.5 indicates that the delinquency rates varied substantially by school, but they did not vary significantly by status grouping
within a given school. The number of self-reported illegal acts for
the institutionalized delinquents was approximately 15, about twice
as high as the self-reported delinquent acts for the students in Schools
I and II. The students in School III reported committing a substantially higher number of delinquent acts than those in Schools I and II,
but not as a great a number as had the institutionalized delinquents.

The rates of reported delinquent behavior increased as the proportion of lower- and working-class youths within the school increased.
A possible explanation is that the conduct norm is established by the
majority; and, even though status groupings within the schools might
differ, the illegal behavior patterns tend to conform to the majority
status grouping. This is particularly apparent in the case of School
III, where 75 percent of the students fell into the "lower and working"
status group. The delinquency rate for the "middle and upper" status
students in School III was higher than in Schools I and II, and close
to that of the "lower and working" status students in School III.

TABLE 13.5

Mean Number of Self-Reported Illegal Acts

| School | Status Groupings | |
	Lower and Working	Middle and Upper
School I	7.13	8.03
School II	7.94	8.02
School III	11.21	10.45
Institution	15.73	14.36

Source: Compiled by the authors.

It has been assumed that middle-class delinquency tends to be
of a less serious nature than lower-class delinquency. Ohlin (1960)
stated that middle-class delinquency is "petty" compared with lower-
class delinquent behavior, and the Myerhoffs (1964) reported that the
violations by middle-class gangs committed in Los Angeles were
more often "mischievous" than violent in nature.

To test this assumption, the offenses self-reported by the youths
were classified as serious or petty. Those offenses that would constitute a crime if committed by an adult were termed "serious," and all
others were considered "petty."

As shown in Table 13.6, the contention that middle-class youths
do not commit serious offenses is not substantiated by these data.
The serious delinquency rate for the students in School I who fell into
the lower-working status grouping was lower than the rate of serious
acts committed by the middle and upper status group of students in that
school. In School II, the rate of serious or petty offenses did not vary
substantially by status groupings within the school. The students in
the lower and working status group in School II had a serious offense
rate of 5.28, while those in the middle and upper status grouping had
an offense rate of 4.5. For School III, in which the students were
predominantly lower and working status, the serious offense rate
was 7.66 for the lower and working status group and 6.18 for the
middle and upper status group. In the institutional sample, the serious offense rate varied little by status grouping, with the lower and
working status youths having 10.5 serious offenses, and the middle
and upper status youths having 10.36.

TABLE 13.6

Distribution of Serious and Petty Offenses

| | Status Grouping | | | |
| | Lower and Working | | Middle and Upper | |
School	Serious	Petty	Serious	Petty
School I	3.93	3.2	6.36	1.67
School II	5.28	2.66	4.5	3.52
School III	7.66	3.55	6.18	4.25
Institution	10.5	5.23	10.36	4.0

Source: Compiled by the authors.

DISCUSSION

The findings of this research tend to support the contentions of those authors who have maintained that a common value orientation exists among youths, regardless of the actual socioeconomic position they hold in the community. Substantial differences between lower and working status and middle and upper status groups did not emerge in this study when their adherence to middle- and lower-class value orientations were examined.

The study found that members of both the lower-working status group and the middle-upper status group committed serious delinquent acts. In fact, youths who would be considered typically "middle class" revealed that they had committed acts similar to those for which the youths in the institutional sample had been arrested and incarcerated. This finding is in line with Hirschi's (1969) assertion that social class status of offenders can result in differences in privilege and in punishment.

An important finding of this research was that the number of offenses committed by youths in a particular school setting was related to the proportion of lower and working status youths in that school, rather than to the status of the individual youths. In the two schools with close to a 50-50 balance of lower-working status and middle-upper status youths, the mean number of self-reported illegal acts was virtually identical for lower-working status and middle-upper status youths within these schools. In the school with 75 percent lower-working status youths and in the institutional sample (90 percent lower-working status) there was a higher mean number of self-reported illegal acts, but again the number was almost identical for lower-working status and middle-upper status youths in each setting.

When the mean number of serious delinquent offenses was considered, it was found that the number of serious offenses committed by the youths in each setting increased as the proportion of lower-working status youths in that setting increased. In the schools with an equal proportion of the two status groupings, the mean numbers of serious offenses were virtually identical. A higher mean number of serious offenses occurred in School III, which had a 75 percent lower-working status population; and the highest mean number of serious offenses occurred within the institutional group. However, the lower-working status youths were not disproportionately responsible for these delinquent acts. In fact, in School I the mean number of such acts committed by middle and upper status youths was higher than for the lower and working status youths; though in all the other settings the proportion of serious offenses committed by youths in each status group was almost exactly the same.

This research tends to confirm the finding of Clark and Wenninger (1963) that the highest rates of serious offenses are committed in settings where lower and working classes predominate. However, their contention that the offenses committed by middle- and upper-class youths are predominantly nuisance offenses was not substantiated by this study.

Although additional research should be undertaken, the findings of this study imply that a youth's socioeconomic position may not be a good predictive indicator of delinquency potential, unless other interrelated variables are considered. In the past, values instilled into a youth in the family, the neighborhood, the peer group, and the school tended to be based on the values and orientations held by a single socioeconomic class. A youth tended to interact predominantly with those of the same socioeconomic class in all these settings.

As communities have become more heterogeneous, school districts have become larger and have consolidated youths from a variety of neighborhoods. The advent of voluntary or forced busing has also caused the social class isolation experienced in the past to break down. In some school systems there can be a convergence of several social class behavior patterns, which struggle for dominance until a particular form of behavior comes to be accepted as the norm. This study found that when the lower-working status students predominated in a school population, the amount of delinquent behavior by students of all socioeconomic classes increased.

REFERENCES

Akers, Ronald L. 1961. "Socio-Economic Status and Delinquent Behavior in Three Akron Schools." Master's thesis, Kent State University.

Clark, John P., and Eugene P. Wenninger. 1963. "Goal Orientations and Illegal Behavior Among Juveniles." Social Forces 47 (October): 49-59.

Cloward, Richard A., and Lloyd E. Ohlin. 1960. Delinquency and Opportunity. Glencoe, Ill.: Free Press.

Cohen, Albert K. 1955. Delinquent Boys. Glencoe, Ill.: Free Press.

Hirschi, Travis. 1969. Causes of Delinquency. Los Angeles: University of California Press.

Merton, Robert K. 1968. "Social Structure and Anomie." American Sociological Review 33 (October): 672-82.

Miller, Walter B. 1958. "Lower Class Culture as a Generating
    Milieu of Gang Delinquency." Journal of Social Issues 14, no.
    3: 5–19.

Myerhoff, Howard L., and Barbara G. Myerhoff. 1964. "Field Ob-
    servations of Middle Class Gangs." Social Forces 42 (March):
    328–36.

Ohlin, Lloyd E. 1960. The Development of Opportunities for Youth.
    New York: Syracuse University Youth Development Center.

Reiss, Albert J. 1965. Occupation and Social Status. New York:
    Free Press.

Reiss, Albert J., and Albert Lewis Rhodes. 1961. "The Distribution
    of Juvenile Delinquency in the Social Class Structure." Ameri-
    can Sociological Review 26 (October): 157–64.

Short, James F., and F. Ivan Nye. 1958. "Extent of Unrecorded
    Juvenile Delinquency: Tentative Conclusion." Journal of Crimi-
    nal Law, Criminology, and Police Science 49 (July–August):
    301–15.

Williams, Robin. 1970. American Society. New York: Knopf.

14

PREVENTING DELINQUENCY BY COMMUNITY ORGANIZATION: A MODEL OF YOUTH DIVERSION IN PUERTO RICO

Joseph P. Fitzpatrick

In January 1970, a community-based delinquency prevention project was inaugurated in Ponce Playa, the port section and one of the poorest neighborhoods of Ponce, the second largest city of Puerto Rico. The project is based on the theory that delinquency can be effectively prevented by community organization that enables the members of a deprived community to develop the competency to provide the supports their children need for healthy development. The project represents a significant adaptation of theory, policy, and program to the cultural differences of Puerto Rico and suggests the importance of being sensitive also to cultural differences in mainland American neighborhoods, where advocacy and community organization may be proposed as important elements of delinquency prevention and correction programs. The project has been enthusiastically praised by officials of the judicial system of Puerto Rico and by the funding agencies in Puerto Rico and on the mainland. The evidence indicates that, if funding were transferred to tax levy monies, it would result in substantial savings for the Commonwealth of Puerto Rico. It provides a model that, with some modification, promises to be an effective alternative to the criminal justice system as well.

DESCRIPTION OF THE PROJECT

Briefly the project, Youth and Community Alerted (JYCA), is a Youth Services Bureau in the Playa, an area of 16,000 residents (10 percent of the population of Ponce) marked for generations by poverty, unemployment, high infant mortality, high dropout rates from school, illness, and delinquency. For years the only community resource in the area was a small clinic, a Dispensario conducted by a group of

Catholic nuns. Through the clinic they came to be well known in the
community, and the community came to be well known by them. Beginning in 1968, with the cooperation of the local residents, local private industry, and some financial assistance from the government,
the Dispensario was able to extend its activities to involve a recreation program, a tutoring program, a job-training program in welding
and commercial sewing, and some social service. Because delinquency
rates in the Playa were the highest of the city of Ponce, efforts began
in the summer of 1969 to inaugurate a delinquency prevention program.
With technical assistance provided by the Youth Development and Delinquency Prevention Administration, of the Department of Health,
Education and Welfare, a proposal was made early in 1970 to the Puerto
Rico Crime Commission for Law Enforcement Assistance Administration action funds for the establishment of a Youth Services Bureau. It
was clear that the problem of juvenile justice in Puerto Rico suffered
from many of the same difficulties as that of the Mainland, and that
the program should seek to divert youths from the juvenile justice
system. The proposal called for a program of youth advocates; the
training of a dozen young people, chosen from the Playa itself, to
intervene in support of children beginning to get into trouble with the
law; a counseling program; expansion of the recreational and tutoring programs; vocational counseling; and community development.
The short-term objective was intensive care for children in danger
of becoming delinquents, particularly the 14-to-18 age group; the
long-term objective was the building of community competence, as
well as the fostering of a sense of confidence that the people there
could do something to protect the interests of themselves and those
of their children.

The project completed its seventh year in January 1977. About
125 youths, characterized as "intensive cases," namely, children
who have committed delinquent acts or who are in serious danger of
committing delinquent acts, are regularly under the care of the advocates and the project staff. In the fifth year of the project, for example, from February to September 1974, 68 new cases were accepted
by the project; 41 cases were terminated. Of the 41 cases terminated,
20 were defined as "successfully" terminated; 12 others of the 41 left
the Playa and came to the U.S. mainland; six others left Ponce for
other sections of Puerto Rico; the other three either refused help or
could not be served by the project. The significance of these figures
does not appear in the enumeration, but in the manner by which the
cases come to the project. In the early years of the project, the great
majority of cases were diverted to the project from the Juvenile
Court. Of the 68 new cases from February to September 1974, only
7 came from the Juvenile Court. The great majority, 53 (80 percent),
came directly from the community. In other words, the community

now brings its troublesome children directly to the project, whereas
previously it would have brought them to the court. One important
feature of the Ponce project is the fact that these "intensive" cases
are known as delinquents or potential delinquents only to the few members of the staff who work with them. For all others, they are simply
a small number of the hundreds of children who are being served by
the project every day. The danger of stigma is almost nonexistent.
In September 1974, for example, 485 children were in sports programs;
577 were in education programs. In fact, the official evaluation of
the project, conducted by a private research team engaged by the
Puerto Rico Crime Commission, counted between 1,300 to 1,700
youths being served per month by the project.

    These achievements and many others reflect an emerging in-
crease of community competence among the people of the Playa.
There is a new spirit of confidence and hope, and enthusiasm for participating in community projects. In the recreation program alone,
adults participate as volunteers; community efforts have raised private funds during recent years; attendance at adult education programs
has increased, as well as the number of people from the Playa attending college. Even more important, a series of related projects have
now been built on the Youth Services Bureau Project. A job training
center has been operating; a program to prevent drug addiction; a
remarkable community health program operates with an annual budget
of over $1 million. It consists of a modern central clinic, a staff of
five full-time doctors, 27 nurses, and 80 women from the Playa
trained to act as liaison between the clinic, three satellite health centers, and the 1,200 to 1,300 families of the Playa served by the program. A supported work program, funded partly by the Ford Foundation and partly by the government of Puerto Rico, has been training
young men in landscape gardening and young women in the health care
of the elderly who are confined to their homes. The total value of
all the projects in 1975 amounted to well over $2 million.

    It is interesting to note that in the Playa there has been a sub-
stantial decrease in the number of juvenile cases dealt with by the
police since the project started. In 1968–69, there were 709 police
interventions in Ponce involving juveniles; 113 of these (19 percent)
were in the Playa. In 1974–75, there were 483 police interventions
involving juveniles, 45 of which (9 percent) were in the Playa. It is
difficult to interpret the meaning of these figures, and it would certainly be rash to suggest that the decline in police interventions is the
result of the activities of the Ponce Playa project. Actually the drop
in police intervention with juveniles in Ponce as a whole is attributed
to the rise of more serious adult crimes and the increased attention
given by police to adults rather than juveniles. And no one can say
whether the figures for the Playa would have increased if the project

had not been in existence. However, one conclusion seems certain. The existence of a stable and effective funding base was a significant influence in the decisions of various other federal and commonwealth agencies to locate projects in the area. The project has also been a significant influence in the reawakening of hope and self-confidence of the community and has given a stability to the community, which enables it to provide for its own children with a skill and sophistication that had not been present before.

What are the implications of the project for theory in the delinquency prevention and correction area?

1. The project is based on the theory that the development of community competence is an effective method of preventing and correcting delinquent behavior;

2. The Ponce project is in the true sense a project of "diversion" and not simply an alternative to conventional processes in the juvenile justice system (briefly, the community has replaced the juvenile court as the effective means of dealing with troubled youth);

3. The community in a very real sense has become the "advocate" for itself and for its children;

4. It represents an adoptation of advocacy to a Puerto Rican situation;

5. It demonstrates a method of assisting juveniles that is far less expensive than the juvenile justice system; and

6. It is applicable to the criminal justice system.

Community Competency and Delinquency Prevention

The project grew out of the theory that inspired the Juvenile Delinquency Prevention and Correction Act of 1968, which called for programs to divert youths from the juvenile justice system to community-based projects, whose staff members could act as advocates for youth in trouble. This policy was recommended by the Report of the President's Commission on Law Enforcement and Administration of Justice (1967), which presented abundant evidence that correctional institutions were neither preventing nor correcting juvenile delinquency; if anything they were contributing to it. Both the report and the legislation were responses to a growing body of theory about delinquency that called to attention not the personality maladjustment of the child needing correction (a conventional view), but flaws in the structure of society in which the youths were growing up and in which the youths had little or no opportunity of access to meaningful adult roles in American society. Cloward and Ohlin (1960) called attention to problems of socializaing children to compete for socioeconomic advance-

ment and then blocking their way to opportunities to compete legiti-
mately; Albert K. Cohen (1955) and Walter B. Miller (1958) called
attention to the subcultures in which delinquency fulfills a positive
function as a reaction of frustrated youth against middle-class society. Martin and Fitzpatrick (1964) called attention to the need for a
new method of assessing the behavior of youth by introducing sociocultural and situational variables into the process. These theories
pointed to the dysfunctions of the juvenile justice system in which the
poor were deprived of opportunities for development and then accused
of delinquency when they resorted to deviant behavior to pursue the interests the society had encouraged them to pursue. Out of this theory
emerged the policy of seeking to provide deprived communities with
the means of developing the competency to provide their children
with supports similar to those provided by middle-class communities
to their youth. The latest official policy based on these theoretical
developments is the Juvenile Justice and Delinquency Prevention Act
of 1974, which emphasizes once again the importance of community-
based projects that divert youth from the juvenile justice system and
seek to provide for youth, in the context of their everyday life, the
supports they need to get started into a meaningful adulthood. The
success of the Ponce Playa Project supports the validity of these
theories.

Diversion Through the Development of Community Competence

Most diversion programs that have been developed during the
past ten years are actually not programs of diversion. The youth remains under the jurisdiction of the court and the Office of Probation
while he is referred to a community-based program, which seeks to
assist him. The youth is still involved with the juvenile justice system; an alternative to confinement is being used. This is quite clear
from the three-volume report, The Challenge of Youth Service Bureaus,
the report of the National Study of Youth Service Bureaus conducted
by the Department of California Youth Authority (1973). The impressive feature of the Ponce Playa Project is the fact that the juvenile
court is largely out of the picture. The great majority of "intensive"
cases now under the care of the project have come to the project
through the community. Furthermore, as indicated above, these
youths under intensive care become simply part of the extensive program involving hundreds of other youths and members of the community. Some of these intensive cases are brought to the project by
parents or relatives; some are located by the staff members who are
advocates; some of them are identified in the routine activities of the

project's programs; some are referred by the school. In other words, the activities of the project have permeated the community; and it has now become the convenient institution that enables the community to provide for its children the attention and support that it was much less capable of providing before the project came into existence.

This makes it difficult to assess the success of the project by conventional methods. Ordinarily evaluators look for case reports, clearly stated criteria by which rehabilitation is identified, objectives to be reached, and indicators that enable the evaluator to determine that the objective has been reached. Even the government is impatient for numbers. But the application of this method is likely to miss the heart of the Ponce Playa project, the role of the project in enabling the community to come alive, to collaborate in the development of a wide range of facilities, from the remarkable community health program to the building of a community center by the barrio residents, and to use this array of facilities as a means of improving its own life and that of its children.

A striking example of this appeared during the past two years, 1974–76. In 1973 the commonwealth government planned a relocation of hundreds of Playa families from a riverbank that was susceptible to repeated flooding. The government built a low-cost housing development on vacant land in the Playa, called it Lirios del Sur (Lilies of the South), relocated hundreds of Playa families together with families from other areas of Ponce, then cleared the land around the river for a flood control project. When the families moved to the new area, signs of disorganization and tension appeared quickly; the building reserved as a community center was misused, partly vandalized, and uncared for. The project staff extended the activities of the project to the new housing development, rented part of the development as a satellite center, and began to transform the lives of the people in Lirios del Sur. The project again becomes the focus around which the community discovers its resources, and marshals them for its own betterment and the betterment of its children.

The Community as Advocate

When the Ponce Playa Project started, there was great difficulty in finding a suitable term in Spanish that could convey the meaning of "advocate" as used on the mainland in reference to delinquency. The term intercessor was finally decided on, someone who intervenes at a strategic moment on behalf of the child, either to provide relevant information to enable people to understand the case, or to assist him in relation to institutions that should be serving him, or by supporting him in a variety of ways. Twelve young people, chosen from the

Playa itself, who understand the life and ways of Playeros (residents of the Playa), and trained in all aspects of the juvenile justice system and the programs of the project, are assigned to the intensive cases as advocates. The particular advocate becomes acquainted with the youth assigned to him (very likely from his own barrio or neighborhood); works with the project staff to identify the problems of the youth; becomes acquainted with parents, friends, and peers; then seeks to be of assistance to the youth and to involve him in many aspects of the project that may be helpful and interesting to the youth: in brief, to fulfill the role of advocate as it is ordinarily understood on the mainland. The National Study of Youth Service Bureaus identified the Ponce Playa program as "the most notable example of advocacy in youth service bureaus." The study also made note of other aspects of advocacy: "In addition, the bureau and its leadership are advocates for community improvements, i.e., better sanitation, drug abuse prevention, and improved educational facilities."

In a paper by Ferre and Fitzpatrick (1972), a detailed description of the project is presented in which the exercise of advocacy is analyzed as an outstanding example of the adaptation of an American mainland idea to a culturally different environment. Advocacy is exercised in a decidedly Puerto Rican style. The article calls attention to the fact that advocacy was not confined to an individual relationship between one advocate and one youth. The youth advocates filtered through the community, linked their activities to all the other activities of the project, particularly to the activities of the community organizers, and catalyzed around themselves a capacity of the community to act as advocate for itself and its children. There is a quality of "totality of life and experience" that characterizes the project; it is not a highly specialized service provided by trained individuals in carefully organized settings. It is a "way of life" developing around the 12 youth advocates and all the other aspects of the project, and resulting in a community environment where the community is relating to all its children, particularly ones getting into trouble, in a very effective way. In other words the youth advocates have not monopolized a function in their own role; they disperse their skill throughout the community in such a way that it enables the community to develop and exercise its competency as its own advocate.

Particular Features of Advocacy in
the Ponce Playa Project

Observers of the project have often questioned whether the characteristics of the project first described are sufficient to explain the success of the project. Probably not. The level of success is cer-

tainly related to a combination of situations and cultural factors prevailing in the project. The role of the Dispensario and its staff of
nuns had prepared over many years an environment of complete confidence among the Playeros in any project the Dispensario would un-
dertake in their behalf. The project was never perceived as something brought into the Playa from outside. The community saw it very
much as their own. It enjoyed complete credibility from the start
and, as Playeros were trained to staff it and it began to provide services for the youth of the Playa, the credibility was confirmed and
even deepened. Furthermore, the director of the project is a woman
of unusual charisma and qualities. A member of one of the most prom-
inent families in Puerto Rico, but living among the poor as one dedi-
cated to them, she has exercised a particular kind of advocacy not unlike that of the influential and wealthy women of the settlement house
days of the last century. She fulfills a very important role, widespread in the Latin world, one which is surprisingly effective when it
is played well—the role of the Patrón, the one who effectively links
the poor and humble with the world of wealth and power for the benefits and services the poor need. Meantime, the residents of the community are being prepared to manage the project on their own. Each
of the units that has been developed around the Youth Service Bureau
has its own board of directors composed largely of members of the
community, which is learning to take responsibilities for the inter-
mediary institutions they have been creating.

Financing

The most impressive feature of the Ponce Playa Project, like
other effective diversion programs, is the substantial saving to the
city, state, or federal governments. As indicated above, at the time
of the official evaluation of the project by evaluators engaged by the
Puerto Rican Crime Commission, the project was serving between
1,300 to 1,700 youths per month. The per capita cost for these children is trifling, less than $200 per child, per year. If only the 125
intensive cases were considered, the per capita cost is still substantially below the cost of maintaining the children in corrective institutions, where the annual cost per child is estimated at $8,000 to
$10,000 per child, per year. In two similar diversion projects in
New York City, the Neighborhood Youth Diversion Program in the
Bronx, New York, and the Placement Prevention Project in the Family Court of the Puerto Rican Family Institute, the savings to city
and state are above a million dollars per year. A proposal has been
submitted to the legislature of Puerto Rico requesting a transfer of
the project to tax levy funds. If this should be done, the government

of Puerto Rico will save large sums of money that would have been
necessary to provide care for the children who are receiving far better care for much lower cost in the project.

Finally, proposals are being prepared to extend the model of
community-based programs for the diversion of young adults from
the criminal justice system. The supported work program mentioned
above, already in progress at the Ponce Playa, is providing job training for young adults, some of whom have been diverted from the criminal justice system. It is important to note that all the trainees in the
first session of this supported work program found employment when
their training was completed. The evidence appears convincing that,
at least at this level of the young adult, the intervention of advocates,
the network of community supports, the preparation for useful employment, the association of the young adults with others involved in
useful and lawful activities would be equally effective in guiding the
young adult toward a healthy, productive adult life.

The experience of the project, therefore, supports the theory
on which it was based, namely that delinquency and crime are frequently the consequence of structural defects in society, that they occur in the absence of a network of intermediate institutions, which
should be the effective link between the youth and the services they
need for development. This constitutes a new definition of an organized and integrated community. In this context, disorganization is
not perceived in terms of the incidence as prevalence of personality
disorders, but rather in terms of institutional dislocation; that is,
either the absence of intermediate structures that link the youths of
a neighborhood to essential services that they need, or the failure of
existing structures to function effectively to promote the interests
of the poor. The integrating factor in progress for the prevention
and correction of delinquency must be the organized community, a
community that has the competency to manage the structures linking
it with the resources and power of the larger society, or the competency to create these structures if they do not exist. At the community level, that is really the capacity to exercise advocacy for itself
and its members, particularly its youth. By achieving this, the community becomes alive and self-confident in its awareness of its power
to create an environment in which youths have assurance that they
will have access to resources they need to enter a productive adult
life.

REFERENCES

California, Department of California Youth Authority. 1973. The
     Challenge of Youth Service Bureaus: Report of the National

Study of Youth Service Bureaus, edited by Alan Breed and George Roberts. Sacramento: California Youth Authority.

Cloward, Richard, and Lloyd Ohlin. 1960. Delinquency and Opportunity. New York: Free Press.

Cohen, Albert. 1955. Delinquent Boys: The Culture of the Gang. Glencoe, Ill.: Free Press.

Ferre, Isolina, and Joseph Fitzpatrick. 1972. "Community Development and Delinquency Prevention, Puerto Rican and Mainland Models." In Politics, Crime and the International Scene, an Inter-American Focus, edited by Freda Adler and G. Miller, pp. 276-81. San Juan, Puerto Rico: North-South Center Press.

Martin, John, and Joseph Fitzpatrick. 1964. Delinquent Behavior: A Redefinition of the Problem. New York: Random House.

Miller, Walter. 1958. "Lower Class Culture as a Generating Milieu of Gang Delinquency." Journal of Social Issues 14, no. 3: 5-19.

President's Commission on Law Enforcement and Administration of Justice. 1967. Report: The Challenge of Crime in a Free Society. Washington, D.C.: U.S. Government Printing Office.

PAUL C. FRIDAY is Associate Professor of Sociology at Western Michigan University. He has taught at the University of Wisconsin and Ohio State University. He is past Vice-President of the American Society of Criminology and the current chair of the International Liaison Committee of the ASC. He was also a Visiting Professor at Westfalia State University in Münster, Germany (1974) and Fulbright scholar at the University of Stockholm, Sweden (1975). Dr. Friday received a B.A. from Drew University in 1964 and an M.A. in 1966 and a Ph.D. in 1970 from the University of Wisconsin at Madison.

V. LORNE STEWART is a Consultant on juvenile justice to the United Nations section on Crime Prevention and Criminal Justice in New York City and a Visiting Fellow of the Center of Criminology, University of Toronto. He is the Vice-President of the International Association of Youth Magistrates. From 1944 through 1973 he was Judge of the Juvenile and Family Court in Toronto, Canada. Dr. Stewart has attended the University of Saskatchewan, the University of Toronto, and the University of Pennsylvania.

CLEMENS BARTOLLAS is Assistant Professor at Sangamon State University, Springfield, Illinois. He has a Ph.D. in Sociology from Ohio State University and a S.T.M. from San Francisco Theological Seminary.

PEDRO R. DAVID is Chairman of the Sociology Department at the University of New Mexico and currently the continental secretary of the International Institute of Sociology. Born in Argentina, Professor David holds advanced degrees in jurisprudence, political science, and sociology, has been a teacher and administrator in the United States and Latin America, and has served as a judge in Argentina.

LEO DAVIDS is Associate Professor at York University in Toronto, Canada. Dr. Davids is also an ordained rabbi. His doctoral research concerned Foster Fathers.

GIDEON FISHMAN is a Lecturer in Sociology at the University of Haifa, Israel. He has a M.A. in Sociology from Carleton University, Ottawa, Canada. He completed his Ph.D. at Ohio State University, specializing in criminology and deviant behavior as well as sociological theory.

JOSEPH D. FITZPATRICK is Professor of Sociology at Fordham University. Dr. Fitzpatrick is the author of several books and received his Ph.D. from Harvard University.

JOHN M. GANDY is Professor on the Faculty of Social Work and Lecturer in the Centre of Criminology at the University of Toronto. He received his D.S.W. from the University of Toronto.

JOHN HALSEY is Researcher with the Crime Prevention Council of Stockholm. He has received a B.A. from Dartmouth College and a Diploma from the International Graduate School in Stockholm.

JOSINE JUNGER-TAS works in the Research and Documentation Center of the Ministry of Justice, The Hague. She also worked for nine years as a researcher at the Centre d'Étude de la Délinquence Juvenile in Brussels. She received her Ph.D. from Groningen State University, Netherlands.

ALAN KIRSCHENBAUM is Technion at the Israel Institute of Technology, Haifa. Born in the United States, he received his B.A. from Yeshiva University, M.A. from Brown University, and Ph.D. from Syracuse University.

JOHN KRATCOSKI is Chairman of the Department of Social Science, Palmyra High School, Palmyra, New Jersey. He is active in the presentation of sociology and applied social science courses in public high schools. He has a M.Ed. from Beaver College and a M.A. from St. Joseph College (Philadelphia).

PETER KRATCOSKI is Associate Professor of Sociology and Criminal Justice Studies at Kent State University where he is also the coordinator of the baccalaureate program in corrections. He received his Ph.D. at Pennsylvania State University.

RACHEL MARKOVSKY is assistant to S. Giora Shoham at Tel Aviv University and is working on her Ph.D., the subject of which is "Criminality and Punishment of Women." Mrs. Markovsky has a degree in law, a M.A. in criminology, and was the first woman pilot in Israel.

PAUL NEJELSKI is Deputy Assistant Attorney General in the Office of Improvement in the Administration of Justice of the U.S. Department of Justice. Mr. Nejelski graduated from Yale Law School.

DAVID SHICHOR teaches in the Department of Sociology at the California State College at San Bernardino. He previously taught at the Institute of Criminology and Criminal Law, Tel Aviv University, and received his Ph. D. from the University of Southern California.

S. GIORA SHOHAM is at present engaged in research at Tel Aviv University. For several years he worked with the District Attorney and Attorney General of Israel, and has represented Israel at many international conferences. Professor Shoham received his L.L.D. at the Hebrew University in Jerusalem.

CHRISTOPHER M. SIEVERDES is Assistant Professor at Clemson University in South Carolina. He received his Ph. D. from Mississippi State University and his M.S. from Virginia Commonwealth University.

YITZHAK STEIN is a Captain in the Israeli army and works within the Social Sciences Framework there. He studied Sociology and Criminology at Bar Ilan University and Criminal Law at Tel Aviv University. He has worked extensively with "Street Corner" groups and delinquent girls.

CHARLES W. THOMAS is Associate Professor in the Department of Sociology at Bowling Green State University. He previously taught at Virginia Commonwealth University and at the College of William and Mary. He received his M.A. and Ph. D. from the University of Kentucky.

LILLY WEISSBROD is presently reading for a Ph. D. at the London School of Economics. She received her M.A. in Sociology from Tel Aviv University. Her M.A. thesis dealt with political representation of ethnic groups in Israel.

CRIMINAL RECIDIVISM IN NEW YORK CITY: An
Evaluation of the Impact of Rehabilitation and Diver-
sion Services
Robert Fishman

ISSUES IN CRIMINAL JUSTICE: Planning and Evaluation
edited by Marc Riedel and
Duncan Chappell

PRISONER EDUCATION: Project NewGate and Other
College Programs
Marjorie J. Seashore,
Steven Haberfeld, with
John Irwin and Keith Baker

REFORM IN CORRECTIONS: Problems and Issues
edited by Harry E. Allen and
Nancy J. Beran

TOWARD A JUST AND EFFECTIVE SENTENCING
SYSTEM: Agenda for Legislative Reform
Pierce O'Donnell,
Michael J. Churgin, and
Dennis E. Curtis

TREATING THE OFFENDER: Problems and Issues
edited by Marc Riedel and
Pedro A. Vales